9-04

P9-CSF-256

FURNITURE
RESTORATION
and renovation

Eva Pascual Miró
Mireia Patiño Coll
Ana Ruiz de Conejo Viloria

DT DECORATIVE TECHNIQUES

684.1
PASC

BARRON'S

Marvin Memorial Library
29 W. Whitney Ave.
Shelby, OH 44875-1252

FURNITURE RESTORATION
and renovation

BARRON'S

Contents

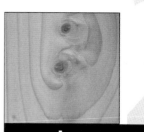

chapter 2
WOOD

**HOW TO RECOGNIZE
AND CARE FOR WOOD**

- What is wood?, 26
- Recognizing different kinds of wood, 26
- Wood parts and pieces, 33
  Boards
  Veneer and inlay wood
  Manufactured shapes
  Commercial marquetry pieces
  Manufactured boards
- Main problems of wood and their
  detection, 36
  Insects
  Mildew
  *The effects of light and changes in
  humidity and temperature*
- Solutions and treatments, 37
  Disinfection

chapter 1
RESTORATION AND RENOVATION: TRENDS AND MATERIALS

**RESTORATION AND RENOVATION:
TWO APPROACHES TO THE SAME END**

- Restoration, 10
- Renovation, 11
- Trends in interior decoration, 11

MATERIALS AND TOOLS

- Materials, 12
  Commonly used materials
  Cleaning and stripping products
  Disinfectants
  Colors and bleaches
  Products for gluing and filling
  Products for finishing
  Auxiliary materials
- Tools, 19
  Cutting tools
  Tools for measuring and marking
  Tools for striking and pulling
  *Tools for making holes, scraping, and
  polishing*
  Tools that apply pressure
  Auxiliary tools
  Power tools

chapter

PROCESSES

STARTING OUT

- Diagnosis, 42
  A bedside table: diagnosis of its general condition
  Checking the condition of the parts
- Project, 43
  Renovating a small table

THE STRUCTURE

- Disassembly, 44
  Disassembling a dresser
  Removing hardware and hinges
- Protecting parts, 45
  Protecting seats and glass pieces
- Filling and gluing, 46
  Repairing with commercial fillers
  Preparing a filler
  Preparing hot glues
  Gluing techniques
  Gluing curved parts
- Assembly, 48
  Assembling an extendable table

PARTS

- Replacing parts, 50
  Adding pulls and lids
  Adding molding
- Replacing pieces, 51
  Replacing a drawer guide

SURFACES

- Stripping, 52
  Stripping with alcohol
  Stripping with caustic soda
  Stripping with commercial gels
  Stripping with sandpaper
  Stripping with a hot air gun
- Cleaning, 54
  Preparing a reanimator
  Cleaning marble
  Cleaning metal
  Cleaning interiors
- Finishes, 56
  Staining
  Retouching
  Varnishing
  Preparing wax
  Preparing shellac
  Antique paint

chapter

RESTORATION

DECORATING INTERIORS WITH RESTORED FURNITURE

- Where to find furniture for restoring, 63
- Plate rack, 64
- Wood chest, 66
- Side table, 68
- Bamboo chair, 72
- Sewing stand, 74
- Wicker umbrella stand, 79
- Wall rack, 82
- Upholstered chair, 88
- Jewelry box, 94
- Writing desk, 97

chapter

RENOVATION

DECORATING INTERIORS WITH RENOVATED FURNITURE

- Where to find and purchase furniture for renovating, 106
- Creating atmosphere with renovated furniture and objects, 107
- Dresser, 108
- Glass cabinet, 112
- Medicine cabinet, 116
- Chair, 118
- Corner stand, 120
- Side table, 122
- Cupboard, 124
- Stool, 130
- Table, 132
- Storage unit for CDs, 136
- Trunk, 138

GLOSSARY, 142

Introduction

Unique and personal environments can be created through the use of restored and renovated furniture. The decorating trends of today favor the use of open spaces that reflect, above all else, the personalities of their users. Decorating with furniture or objects that have been restored can create a unique and innovative atmosphere. The information in this book will be useful for both professionals and beginners. For the former it will be a source of information for their specific needs. And for the latter it will serve both as a reference manual and as a guide to direct them through the steps and processes of the projects. Readers will be able to choose the chapter or subject that interests them, based on their needs and experience. The first and second chapters discuss the materials and tools used for the projects, giving special attention to the different types of woods and their problems and solutions. The third chapter explains the most common methods used in the restoration and renovation of furniture, offering solutions to the most common problems. Beginning with chapter four, the restoration and renovation of several types of furniture and objects made of different materials are explained in step-by-step examples. The group of examples are unique because of the nature of the pieces, but the solutions and systems are easily applied to any project one may wish to attempt. We hope that this book, written by a team of professionals, will be used as a guide for beginners in this field and as a reference source for those with experience.

Eva Pascual, Mireia Patiño, and Ana Ruiz de Conejo

Restoration and renovation: trends and materials

Furniture is the base on which the decoration of interiors is
built. The selection of furniture and its arrangement in a space
creates an image and forms a unique atmosphere in any room.
In many cases, the pieces of furniture will define the use of
the space, whereas the objects will reinforce the aesthetics of
the environment. Interior decoration is based on the correct
selection of objects and furniture to fulfill personal needs
and taste. Through restoration and renovation, we are able
to create unique pieces that reflect our taste and personality,
unlike the uniformity inherent in manufactured pieces. Our
creativity, in the case of renovation, and our taste and
criteria, in the case of restoration, will be the only factors for
our projects.

Restoration and renovation: two approaches to the same end

Although restoration and renovation are different processes that result in different solutions, these processes share the same purpose: to create unique pieces. This purpose can be achieved by returning a furniture piece or object to its original appearance through restoration or by radically transforming its look through renovation. Either approach will contribute a different piece, which will become a part of our living space.

Restoration

The restoration of any object implies bringing back its original qualities and appearance. Every restoration project is guided by specific principles. The first thing to keep in mind, which will guide us through the project, is the importance of identifying the problems and requirements of the restoration. Research and study of the typology, materials, and construction techniques of the object are necessary. Only in this way can we establish the appropriate solutions for a complete restoration.

Restored furniture and objects should be able to fulfill the function for which they were created. It is important to preserve as many of the original elements as possible, only replacing them when their proper use or function has been altered. Accessories—such as marble tops, pulls, keyholes and mirrors—should be preserved, giving them only a good cleaning. Whenever possible, a repair should be reversible.

Because the restoration process should not affect the quality of the object, the workmanship and the quality of the materials used should maintain the value of that object. The finish applied to the wood should be similar to the original. Parts of other furniture or unnecessary objects or creative finishes that are different from the original should not be used. Restoration does not imply transformation of the exterior of the object; on the contrary, the integrity of each part and of the object as a whole should be greatly respected.

An old piece of office furniture decorates the corner of a room. This space, very narrow and located between two doorways, was difficult to decorate. The small piece of furniture helped to resolve the problem.

Renovation

The renovation of a piece of furniture or an object implies the transformation and adjustment of its appearance and structure to adapt it to our taste and needs. Renovation, as opposed to restoration, has no formal or material restrictions, and the extent of the project is limited only by skill and imagination. Any process or solution is allowed in a renovation project, no matter how innovative, although it is necessary to keep certain things in mind.

The first step is to evaluate the general condition of the piece and the possibilities that it offers for transformation. This step always depends on our skills and capability for planning and carrying out the solutions. The tasks that are performed in each project are usually unique; therefore, it is important to plan them beforehand.

Renovating the exterior of furniture or objects requires changing some parts and adding new ones made of various materials. As parts of greater or lesser importance are removed or added, the use of furniture and objects is transformed.

The renovation of this table resulted in a piece of furniture with a unique personality.

Trends in interior decoration

The latest trends in interior decoration place special emphasis on the return to warm environments, with a focus on materials and textures, and spaces that are better adapted to the particular needs of its users. Restoring and renovating our own furniture allows us to decorate our environment in a distinct and personal way. Natural materials like wood, wicker, cane, raw fabrics, slate, and marble are being brought back and newly appreciated, as opposed to the synthetic materials that were so popular in the past decades. Handcrafted pieces are now in great demand, because they add authenticity and tradition to our surroundings. Furniture and objects that are handcrafted in other countries with cultures different from our own bring to us a different and enriching reality that increases their decorative value. Fresh and informal surroundings are preferred, and practicality and comfort are a priority, resulting in spaces that can be lived in, not just contemplated or admired. Antique furniture and pieces with a rustic look are considered special, and they find a place in favored areas. Antiques are combined with modern pieces that are almost avant-garde.

Materials and tools

Renovation and restoration projects require the use of different materials and tools. The various steps in any project require the use of common materials as well as materials that are specialized and specific to each case.

Most of the tools that are used come from the carpentry trade, but tools that are typically used in art or for the restoration of other materials are also used.

Materials

Innumerable materials are available for use in the different phases of restoration and renovation. Because each project is unique, the processes and materials used are usually exclusive to it. However, because certain materials are used for nearly all projects, we will offer the following brief overview of them. Their correct handling and use will help us achieve the desired results, so it is very important to understand their nature, composition, and properties.

Cotton cloths.

Commonly used materials

• Cleaning materials

Cleaning materials are used in all projects. Cotton cloths and cotton strands are sold by the bag. They are used for applying various products as well as for removing them and for cleaning surfaces, because they can get into hard-to-reach corners.

A homemade swab is the most practical tool for cleaning surfaces that are delicate or that have nooks and crannies. It is made like this: A piece of cotton is rolled on the end of a long wood stick of medium thickness; one part of the stick is held with one hand, and the other end of the stick is grasped with the other. Next, the stick is rotated while the cotton is wrapped and pulled tight in the opposite direction. The cotton will be firmly attached to the stick, which will serve as a handle.

Cotton cloths can be used for cleaning surfaces, for polishing wax finishes on wood, and for making finishing pads. The fabric should be lint-free.

Cotton and sticks for making a swab.

Vegetable fibers, such as sparto grass, are used for cleaning and for removing wood grain that has been raised by water. It is also used as filler for upholstery.

Cotton strands.

Vegetable fibers (sparto grass).

• **Material for templates**

Carbon paper and graph paper will be needed for making templates of molding or shapes that must be painted or cut out of wood.

• **Applicators**

Different applicators are used for restoration and renovation projects, for painting, varnishing, applying shellac, retouching, and gluing. Flat, wide brushes are commonly used for applying glue, varnish, and occasionally shellac. Brushes of different brands, materials, and shapes are commercially available, each appropriate for a specific task.

• **Carpentry materials**

Some carpentry tasks must be carried out in nearly every restoration and renovation project. Therefore, it is necessary to have nails and brads, screws, needles, tacks, and hooks for use with steel, wood, and upholstery. (Brads can be used in those cases where we do not wish to see the head of a fastener.) Tacks are used in upholstery to attach the webbing and the twine that hold the springs in place. Hooks bent at a right angle at one end with or without screw threads at the other can be used for hanging objects.

• **Adhesive tape**

Adhesive, or masking, tape is used to protect surfaces and objects that cannot be removed—for example, when applying paint and varnish. Plastic packing tape is the most appropriate adhesive tape for holding the edges of the plastic when making a disinfecting bag.

• **Plastic**

Plastic is used for making disinfecting bags. Polyethylene is ideal for this task because it is inert, it does not release noxious fumes, and it is resistant to disinfectant products.

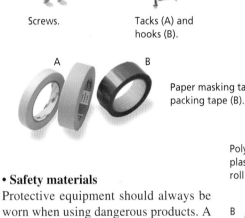

A   B

Carbon paper (A) and graph paper (B).

Applicators: sable brushes (A), paint brushes (B), and wide brushes (C).

B

A

Screws.

Tacks (A) and hooks (B).

Nails and brads.

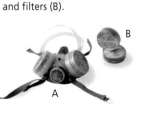

A   B

Paper masking tape (A) and plastic packing tape (B).

Polyethylene (A) and plastic food wrap in a roll (B).

B   A

• **Safety materials**

Protective equipment should always be worn when using dangerous products. A respirator is good protection for dust and noxious fumes. Never use filters or masks that have passed their date of expiration. Safety glasses are especially important when stripping paint and finishes. Neoprene gloves are necessary when working with irritants like paint strippers and caustic soda.

A

B

C

Neoprene gloves (A), cloth and leather gloves (B), cloth gloves with a nonslip covering (C).

Respirator with interchangeable filters (A) and filters (B).

Disposable respirator for dust and fumes.

B

A

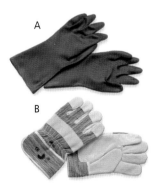

A

B

C

Disposable dust masks.

Safety glasses.

Cleaning and stripping products

• Sandpaper and sanding blocks

The secret of a good finish—whether varnished, painted, shellacked, or waxed—is good sanding, so it is important to use the right sandpaper for each job. Heavy grit sandpaper is used for deep sanding surfaces that are in poor condition. Fine sandpaper is used to polish the wood before the finish is applied. Sandpaper is also used in some painting techniques to simulate an antique finish. It is a good idea to use a sanding block with sandpaper wrapped around it so that pressure is applied evenly when performing this task. Sanding sponges, with their rough surfaces, are best used for curved or uneven surfaces.

• Steel wool

Steel wool is used to remove or polish varnish and, in certain artistic techniques, to create an old or worn look. It is available in different grades, from the roughest (0) to the finest (0000), and is sold in small bags or in rolls for industrial use.

• Cleaners

A grease-cutting mixture of water, neutral soap, and ammonia can be used to clean the surfaces of furniture or objects. Neutral soap has a pH of 7, and it will not damage the wood when used as an ingredient or by itself. Ammonia is a powerful cleaner, and it is used to activate bleaching. When working with ammonia, a respirator specified for ammonia fumes should be used as a safety measure.

• Stripping agents

Stripping agents are used to remove varnish or paint finishes from furniture. Alcohol is very effective for stripping old varnish made with shellac, yet it is harmless and quite inexpensive. Commercial strippers remove paint and varnish from any type of furniture; however, because they are chemical products, they should be handled with caution (gloves, a respirator, and safety glasses) and used according to the manufacturer's instructions. Caustic soda diluted in water can be used to remove paint and varnish from solid pinewood, using the same precautions as with other stripping agents.

• Special cleaning products

Cleaning anything other than wood requires the use of special products and techniques. Certain types of metals covered with a patina can be cleaned by using a mixture of vegetable oil and tripoli. Tripoli is a material that comes from limestone that is used as a polish. Another useful product is rottenstone, a finely ground limestone that is used as a component in cleaning mixtures, and that is also used to fill the pores of wood when applying certain finishes.

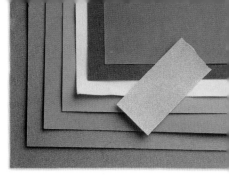

Different types of sandpaper.

Sanding blocks.

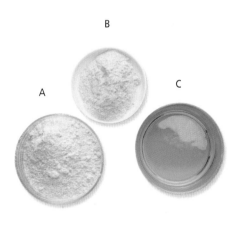

Stripping gel (A), caustic soda (B), and cleaning pad (C).

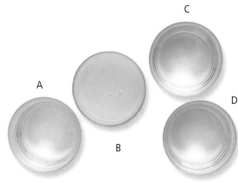

Rottenstone (A), tripoli (B), and vegetable oil (C).

Steel wool.

Alcohol (A), neutral liquid soap (B), distilled water (C), and ammonia (D).

Disinfectants

• Commercial disinfectants

A disinfecting treatment should be applied if there is evidence of insects. Disinfectants are liquids that are applied to the wood and injected into the holes that insects have left. Because these products are highly toxic, gloves and a respirator for fumes should be worn when handling them, and the work should be done in a well-ventilated place.

• Thymol

Thymol is a disinfectant that is obtained from thyme and other plants. It is a powerful antifungal that is used in liquid form dissolved in alcohol.

• Paradichlorobenzine

Paradichlorobenzine is the active ingredient in mothballs and pellets. It is a solid, but its effect, which last only until the application is stopped, comes from its fumes.

Paradichlorobenzine (A), thymol (B), and a commercial liquid disinfectant (C).

Colors and bleaches

• Pigments

Pigments are the colored substances to which no binder or vehicle has been added—that is to say, before they are made into paint. They can be organic or inorganic, depending on the material from which they are made. They are mainly used for coloring waxes, paints, and varnish.

• Colors

Universal colors are liquid artistic pastes that contain soluble pigments. They are used to color or change the tone of existing paints. Different types of dyes can be used to stain wood: water-based anilines, alcohol-based anilines, asphalt, or walnut stain. Anilines are synthetic dyes; the water-based dyes are the easiest to use, although they have the disadvantage of raising the grain of the wood. They are prepared by dissolving the aniline in hot water and shaking it thoroughly. Asphalt is a deep brown-colored dye that covers thoroughly with great color. Walnut stain is an extract of the walnut shell that is dissolved in water and gives the wood a toasted brown color.

Pigments.

• Bleaches

Oxalic acid is prepared for use by putting a large portion of oxalic crystals in hot water, so much so that an undissolved layer of product remains in the bottom of the container. The solution is then applied to the appropriate surface. When it has dried, the surface is washed with a generous amount of flowing water until the oxalic acid is completely removed. A respirator and safety glasses are required while working with this solution.

Another strong bleaching agent is hydrogen peroxide mixed at 30 parts per 100 or 110, also called concentrated hydrogen peroxide. It is a good idea to rinse the object with tap water after the desired tone has been achieved.

Various universal colors.

Hydrogen peroxide (A) and oxalic acid (B).

Dyes for wood: aniline with solvent (A), asphalt (B), aniline with water (C), aniline with alcohol (D), and walnut stain (E).

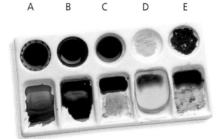

Products for gluing and filling

• Waxes and lacquers

Hard waxes are sold in bar form, in a wide range of colors that can be adapted to any color of wood. They are used to fill small defects and to cover holes that insects have left. Lacquers are used for filling and hiding somewhat larger defects found on the surface of the wood. They are heated and applied while in a liquid state. They solidify quickly, and result in a hard and shiny surface, which makes them good for filling in areas of missing wood that has already been finished.

Wax in bar form.

• Glues and adhesives

Many different adhesives can be used in restoration and renovation. The most common are white carpenter's glue, cyanoacrylate glue, fast-drying adhesives, rabbit skin glue, and animal hide glue. White carpenter's glue, a water-soluble polyvinyl acetate, is the most commonly used. A quick-drying glue with a cyanoacrylate base can be used for small joints and points of contact. Fast-drying adhesives are useful for temporary joints because they can be easily removed with acetone. Animal glues like hide glue or rabbit skin glue are prepared and applied hot, and their use is restricted to restoration projects.

Lacquer in bar form.

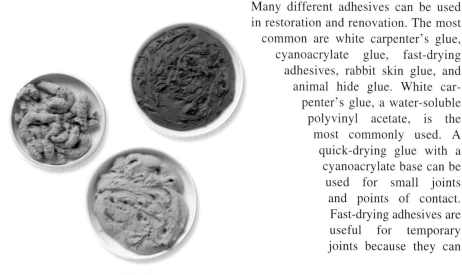

Putties.

• Putties

These products are sold in paste form and are used to cover and fill defects or cracks. When dry, they acquire a texture and feel similar to the wood. Some types of putty (when dry) can be stained and worked as if they were wood.

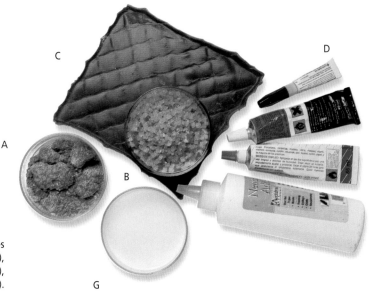

Adhesives: animal hide glue (A), rabbit skin glue granules (B), rabbit skin glue in sheets (C), cyanoacrylate glue (D), fast-drying adhesives (E), neutral polyvinyl acetate glue (F), and carpenter's glue (G).

Shellac in flake form.

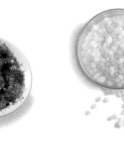

Beeswax.

Wax powder (A), tinted wax (B), liquid wax (C), and paste waxes (D).

Products for finishing

• Shellac

Shellac is a secretion of the lac beetle that lives on different kinds of trees in India and Thailand; it is the only resin of animal origin. It is available in flakes and is soluble in alcohol. A shellac finish is glossy and of high quality, but very delicate.

• Waxes

Waxes are combinations of animal, vegetable, and/or mineral waxes that are mixed with a solvent to create a solid that is smooth to the touch. There are many varieties of furniture wax on the market, including liquid, powdered, paste, pure beeswax, clear, natural color, and tinted. They impart a satin finish to the wood.

• Retouching products

Color markers matching the different woods that are most commonly used in furniture manufacturing are used to retouch small areas after the projects are finished. The project can also be touched up with a brush and solvent-based tint that will not raise the grain of the wood and that is highly resistant to light. Commercial repair colors are used to restore the tone of the wood, to correct small color defects, and to clean surfaces.

• Paint

Enamels and plastic-based paints, both commercially made, are the most common types used for decorating furniture and objects. Enamel is a paint that is manufactured from synthetic oily varnishes with a solvent base that imparts a smooth, glossy finish. Plastic paints are made from vinyl, acrylic, or polyester resins, and they have a water base. Oil paints are used for small decorative motifs and in aging techniques for coloring varnish.

• Varnishes and oils

Varnishes are liquids made of a medium that carries different dissolved resin or gum substances. They are applied in thin coats and will protect the surface of the wood once they have dried. They are sold in liquid or aerosol form; glossy, matte, or satin finishes; and in different colors as well as for protecting different materials, including paint, wood, and metal. Wood filler is a nitrocellulose varnish that covers the pores of the wood, creating a finish that is easily scratched. It is toxic, so a respirator and neoprene gloves must be used. Linseed oil is a liquid that is obtained from pressing ground flaxseeds. It takes 3 to 4 days to dry, and dries from the outside in, first forming a hard outer layer. It is a natural, nontoxic product that imparts a deep glossy finish to the wood.

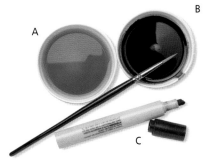

Commercial repair color (A) and solvent-based color (B), and a retouching marker (C).

Enamel (A), oil-based paint (B), and plastic-based paint (C).

Varnish for metals (A), acrylic varnish (B), water-based varnish (C), filler (D), and linseed oil (E).

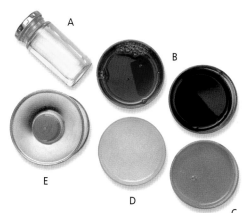

Auxiliary materials

• Upholstery materials

Some restoration and renovation projects require the use of special processes that are typical of other crafts—for example, upholstery. Various materials are used in upholstery work. Needles (curved, longer, and thicker than regular ones) are used for stitching the springs and filled fabrics. Heavy thread is used for sewing and firmly joining together parts of the upholstery. Twine is used to tie the springs. Webbing strips made of strong fabric are attached to the frame to become the underlying framework of the upholstery. The springs add shape and comfort to seats. Burlap or cotton fabric is used to cover and hold the various layers of stuffing. The most common stuffing materials are polyester batting, vegetable fibers, or foam rubber. The latter is sometimes used also for certain decorative painting techniques to make small stamps.

• Hardware

Hardware pieces—other than the regular nails, brads, and screws—are used in most renovation projects. New parts or mechanisms are rarely added when restoring a piece of furniture or an object. The most commonly used hardware elements are drawer pulls, rings, corner brackets, hinges, locks, and keyholes. Wheels, because of their frequent use, are commonly replaced in restorations and renovations of furniture and objects.

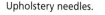

Upholstery needles.

Webbing.

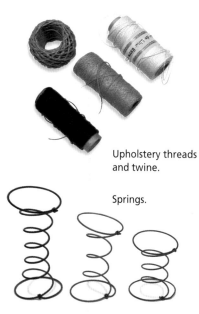

Upholstery threads and twine.

Springs.

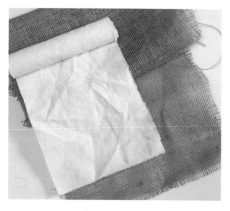

Samples of cotton fabric and burlap.

• Other materials

Syringes are useful for applying disinfectant and other liquid substances into wood, injecting white glue into difficult-to-reach joints, and so on. They are available in different sizes and manufactured with different materials, which makes them useful for any application. Sponges are used for cleaning, applying decorative coatings, and creating effects on paint that is still wet.

Paint companies make color sample cards, which show the range of tones and shades catalogued in order. The cards can be used as a guide for planning and choosing the range of paint colors that are to be used.

Different types of syringes.

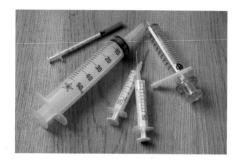

Sponge.

Wheels.

A

B

C

Lock (A), hinges (B), and corners (C).

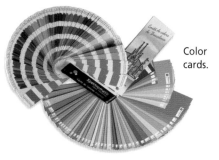

Color cards.

Tools

The tools that can be used for restoration and renovation projects are as varied as the techniques that can be used. Many of the tools are used for other decorative techniques and various crafts like carpentry, upholstery, and decorative painting. Other types of tools commonly used in restoration are also used for restoring paper or paint. It is important to know the uses of each tool in order to choose the one that is appropriate for the project.

Cutting tools

• Scissors, cutting blades, and craft knife
These tools are used for cutting different shapes and materials with more or less precision: sheet metal, templates, and stamps for example.

• Back saw and piercing saw
The back saw, which is named for the reinforcement it has along the back edge, is used for fine and precision cutting. The piercing saw, which consists of a metal frame that holds a very fine blade in a vertical position, is mainly used for marquetry work.

• Plane
The plane consists of a wood block with a slot where an angled blade is held in place by a wedge. It is used for smoothing and removing material from the wood. Metal planes are more precise than wood planes.

• Chisel
The chisel is a tool with a horizontal steel blade at one end and a handle, usually made of wood. Its width ranges from $\frac{3}{16}$ to $1\frac{1}{2}$ inches (4 to 40 mm). It is used for cutting holes and removing wood.

• Miter box
A miter box is made of three pieces of wood in a U shape. The sides have grooves to guide the movement of a saw blade, helping it cut molding and small pieces at a 45- or 90-degree angle.

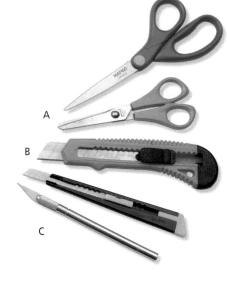

Scissors (A), cutting blades (B), and craft knife (C).

Metal plane.

Back saw and miter box.

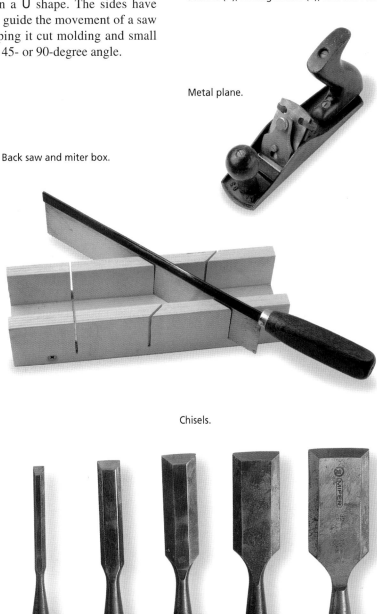

Piercing saw.

Chisels.

Tools for measuring and marking

• Measuring instruments

It is a good idea to have several different measuring instruments: a measuring tape and a ruler for taking measures, a square and triangle for checking right angles, and a scale for transferring details to scale. Calipers are used for taking very precise measurements; they consist of a graduated rule with a square angle at one end that slides against another graduated scale.

• Drawing instruments

Drawing instruments are necessary for constructing templates, creating original drawings that later will be transferred to the object and copied, and transferring already existing designs.

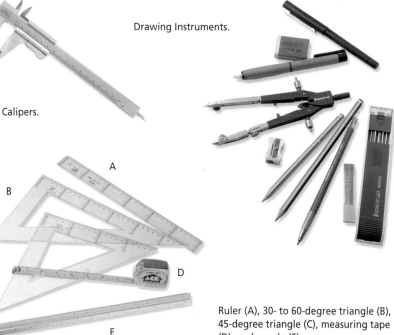

Drawing Instruments.

Calipers.

Ruler (A), 30- to 60-degree triangle (B), 45-degree triangle (C), measuring tape (D), and a scale (E).

Tools for striking and pulling

• Hammers and mallets

Hammers are used for driving nails, striking, and performing those tasks that cannot be done with the force of the hand alone. The mallet is mainly used for striking the handles of cutting tools and tapping together joints and frames. A nylon-headed hammer is used to nail delicate pieces and prevent marring of the wood surface. The upholsterer's hammer is used for driving and pulling the tacks that hold the fabric in place.

• Nail set

The nail set is a steel cylinder that is tapered and has a flat point. It is used to hide brads and finishing nails by sinking them below the surface of the wood.

• Pincers and pliers

Pincers, which are made of two pieces of iron or steel joined by a bolt, are used for pulling and cutting nails. Pliers are similar to pincers, but the ends are conical or squared; they are used for twisting and cutting wire.

• Nail puller

The nail puller is a steel bar used as a lever with a handle at one end and claw at the other. It is used to grasp the heads of nails and pull them.

Upholsterer's hammer.

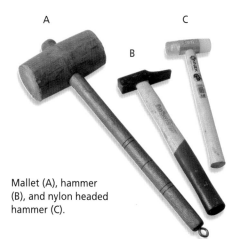

Mallet (A), hammer (B), and nylon headed hammer (C).

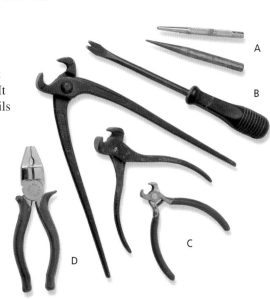

Nail sets (A), nail puller (B), pincers (C), and pliers (D).

Tools for making holes, scraping, and polishing

• Gimlet
The gimlet is used for making small holes. It consists of a steel rod with a threaded, conical tip and a wood handle for turning the tool.

• Hand drill
A hand drill is a small drill that would almost fit in a pocket. A bit is held in the chuck, which rotates as the handle is pushed down. It is used to drill small holes.

• Scraper blades and paint scrapers
The paint scraper is used for removing varnish during the stripping process. Scraper blades are made of high-quality, semihard tempered steel, and are usually rectangular, although they come in different shapes that will adapt to all surfaces. They are used for polishing surfaces using the cutting burr that is on the long edges.

• Nooker knife
The nooker knife has a sharply pointed steel rod at one end and a wood handle at the other end. It is used for scraping in grooves that larger tools cannot reach, polishing wood, or removing varnish. Scrapers are used for scraping larger areas.

• Files
Files are tools made of tempered steel, with grooved faces that can remove small splinters of wood. Rasps are a type of file that have large triangular teeth.

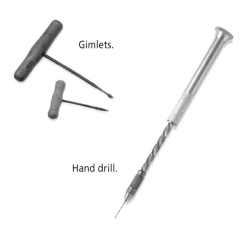
Gimlets.

Hand drill.

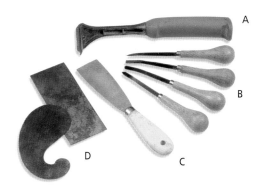
Scraper (A), nooker knives (B), paint scraper (C), and scraper blades (D).

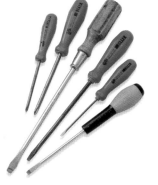

Rasps (A) and files (B).

Tools that apply pressure

• Screwdrivers
Screwdrivers have a hard steel rod shaped like a particular type of screw at one end and a plastic or wood handle at the other. They are used for driving and removing screws.

• Clamps
Clamps are steel or plastic instruments that have two stops, one adjustable and the other fixed. They are used for holding and applying pressure to objects.

• Bench vise
The function of the bench vise is to hold objects to the work surface. The bench vise is clamped to the work surface from the bottom.

• Canvas-stretching pliers
Canvas-stretching pliers, which are made of steel, have rectangular jaws and teeth that nest perfectly when closed. They are used for holding and stretching canvas, webbing, and fabric.

Canvas-stretching pliers.

Clamps.

Screwdrivers.

Bench vise.

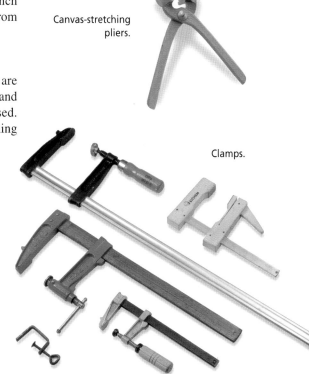

Auxiliary tools

• Utensils for mixing

It is a good idea to have various types of utensils for mixing and dispensing products: wood spoons and spatulas for stirring mixtures that contain solvent that could attack metal, sticks for stirring hot glue, and metal spatulas for applying pastes or dispensing small quantities of material.

• Double boiler

A double boiler slowly and evenly heats material in a container that is partially submerged in water that is held in a larger container. An electric hot plate or burner is required (never gas because it is too dangerous), as is a shallow, wide container for the water and a clay pot or a wide-mouthed container for diluting and heating the different materials.

• Measuring instruments

It is necessary to measure and weigh the different materials used for making various mixtures, including stains and disinfectants. Graduated volumetric measures are used for measuring liquid volume, and the most accurate are graduated laboratory glass beakers. A mechanical or digital scale is used for weighing solids.

• Containers

Containers are used for mixing, saving leftover paint, and cleaning brushes. It is a good idea to have an assortment of different kinds of jars, made of different materials, with lids and containers of different shapes. Care should be taken when pouring any kind of solvent into a plastic container, because it could melt, emit toxic substances, or both.

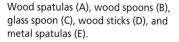

Wood spatulas (A), wood spoons (B), glass spoon (C), wood sticks (D), and metal spatulas (E).

• Brushes

Brushes are used for cleaning and polishing. Shoe brushes with soft bristles are useful for buffing surfaces that are curved or that have grooves and carvings. Toothbrushes are best for cleaning and scrubbing delicate materials like wicker. The metal brushes that are sold for cleaning suede leather are useful for cleaning metal objects and parts. Brushes with natural vegetable fiber bristles are used for cleaning certain parts of furniture or scrubbing surfaces during the stripping process.

Double boiler: burner and containers.

Graduated bottle (A), graduated test tube (B), graduated beaker (C), and scale (D).

Different types of containers.

Brushes: brush with vegetable fiber bristles (A), toothbrush (B), metal brush (C), and shoe brush (D).

Power tools

• Drill

The power drill is used for making holes. Drill bits can be changed quickly and easily, depending on the item being drilled—whether it is wood, masonry, or metal—and the size of the hole desired.

• Hot air gun

The hot air gun is used for removing heavy layers of paint and is useful on vertical surfaces. It blows hot air, and some models have flow and temperature controls.

• Sander

The electric sander is used for smoothing large surfaces that are in poor condition. Different kinds of abrasive papers can be used with the sander.

• Rotary tool

A rotary tool is a small tool with a chuck at one end that can be fitted with various grinding heads, disks, and bits, among other things. Because of the powerful motor, the bits rotate at a high speed to quickly and efficiently complete tasks.

• Handheld torch and electric burn-in knife

The small handheld torch consists of a gas canister with a burner tip at one end. It is used for melting wax and lacquer.

The electric burn-in knife has a temperature control and certain models have interchangeable tips. It is useful for applying hot wax or lacquer and for repairing dents.

Power drill.

Hot air gun.

Electric sander.

Electric burn-in knife.

Small gas torch.

Rotary tool.

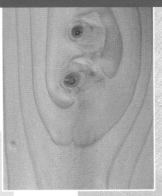

2 Wood

Wood
has traditionally been the primary material used for making furniture.
Even though many materials are used for this purpose today, wood continues to be the best choice in terms
of quality and the most popular. Whether the project is furniture
restoration or renovation, it is necessary to become very familiar
with the structure and properties of wood and to be able to identify
most of its species. It is also important to know the shapes and forms
of wood that are available and which of them can be cut to order.
Wood is an organic material, and as such it has its own special
problems. In order to identify and prevent these problems
beforehand, it is necessary to understand and
know how to remedy them.

How to recognize and care for wood

Wood has traditionally been the primary material used to make furniture, decorative objects, and structural elements for interiors. For the last several decades, other materials that have light structures and are resistant to wear and easy to clean have been used in the manufacture of inexpensive furniture and decorative pieces. However, wood continues to be much appreciated for its aesthetic value.

What is wood?

Wood is made up of fibers that serve as support and allow water and nutrients to circulate in large plants, such as trees and bushes. It also has varying quantities of materials (depending on the species) like cellulose, lignite (lignin), resin, starch, tannins, and sugars. Wood is, therefore, a living thing, just like the tree or bush that it came from, and it goes through a series of changes that cause it to grow, develop, and die.

Cut wood is dried and treated for later use in the construction of furniture or various objects. However, its main characteristic, being an organic material that was once alive, affects its use, restoration, and conservation. The different materials it is made of and its internal structure may undergo several changes, depending on environmental factors, which can partially or even entirely transform its properties, including color, texture, hardness, flexibility, and resistance. Different types of wood react in different ways to the adverse factors in the surrounding environment, depending on the nature of the wood and the way in which it was worked as well as the substances used to modify it and seal it.

Recognizing different kinds of wood

The first thing that should be taken into account when restoring or renovating a piece of furniture is the kind of wood that was used in its construction. This identification helps us determine if the renovations or intended decorative solutions are truly viable. It allows us to know how the wood will react to external agents and, therefore, what problems we may encounter. This way, the most adequate method of restoration, processes, finish, and conservation techniques for the object can be established.

There are innumerable species of trees and bushes that can be used to construct furniture; their use varies by country and region. Here we will present the most common ones in order to establish a basic repertoire that will help as a guide for identifying different woods. Sometimes, however, problems or doubts can arise, especially at the beginning. This is quite normal, and can only be overcome by years of practice and experience. Do not hesitate to consult a professional woodworker, who will surely be able to correctly identify the wood and share his or her knowledge of it.

• **Birch.** *Betula pendula.*
Betula alba. Betula verrucosa
A softwood of a yellowish to reddish white color, with a short, compact grain. Its high quality veneers are used for plywood.

• **Fir.** *Abies alba*
A soft, resinous white-colored wood with a long, straight grain. Strong contrast between the spring wood and autumn wood. It has wide annual rings and dark knots.

• **Poplar.** *Populus alba*
A yellowish white- to gray-colored softwood that is easy to work. Not resistant to insects and humidity, with a tendency to crack. It is used for making the framework of furniture.

• **Maple.** *Acer campestre*
A light-colored fine-grained wood. Not very resistant to insects and outdoor weather. It is used for making furniture.

• **Bird's eye maple.** *Acer campestre*
It owes its name to the characteristic pattern of knots. This wood comes from the root of the maple. It is cut into sheets for use as veneer.

• **Balsa.** *Ochoroma lagopus*
This wood is soft, light, not very dense with a lustrous pink-beige to light straw color, with a straight, even grain. It is used for making supports, insulation, and models.

Birch.

Fir.

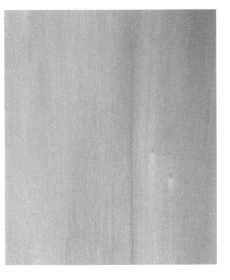
Poplar.

Maple.

Bird's eye maple.

Balsa.

• **Boxwood.** *Buxus sempervirens*
A hard, dense, even-grained wood with a strong yellow color. It is used for making utensils and tool handles. High-quality sheets and fillets are also cut for use in inlay and marquetry for beautiful ornamental effects.

• **Mahogany.** *Swietenia*
A hardwood with a characteristic dark red color with a curved and even grain that is dense and durable. It is very resistant to insects. Used in fine wood-working, it is also used for inlay, marquetry, and veneering work. Today this species is threatened with extinction because of intensive logging in tropical forests.

• **Mahogany crotch.** *Swietenia*
This is veneer that comes from the crotch of the tree where the trunk is divided. If it is cut perpendicular to the trunk, the characteristic lustrous feather-like grain pattern can be seen.

• **Chestnut.** *Castanea sativa*
A strong, flexible hardwood with a reddish ochre color and open grain. It is not very resistant to insects. It stays in good condition in water but tends to split when it comes in contact with air.

• **Cedar.** *Cedrus atlantica*
An aromatic, pinkish wood with irregular growth rings and sometimes knots. It is easy to work and carve.

• **Cherry.** *Prunus avium*
This is quite a hard wood, with a characteristic light brown color and straight grain. It is used by woodworkers to construct high-quality furniture, and is cut into sheets for marquetry and veneering. It is easy to stain and polish.

Boxwood.

Mahogany.

Mahogany crotch.

Chestnut.

Cedar.

Cherry.

Cypress.

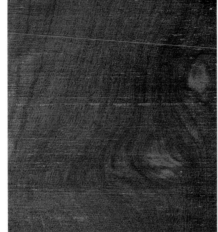

Ebony.

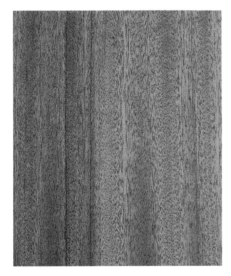

African walnut.

Eucalyptus.

Chilean eucalyptus.

Ash.

• **Cypress.** *Cupressus sempervirens*
Hard, resinous, and aromatic, this wood is pale with a reddish grain. Its high resin content makes it very resilient and long lasting.

• **Ebony.** *Diospyros*
A very hard wood with a fine grain that is heavy and intensely black in color. Difficult to work, it is used for wood turning and inlay work. The species is in danger of extinction because of over-exploitation of the forest.

• **African walnut.** *Lovoa klaineana*
A fairly hard wood that is not very dense, reddish gray to dark brown in color with iridescence and a fine texture. It is very durable and resistant to rot. Somewhat difficult to work and finish, it is used for making paneling and for veneer on furniture.

• **Eucalyptus.** *Eucaliptus*
A very hard and strong wood, light brown to gray with interwoven fibers. Fine textured, it is dense but very light. Stable and durable, it is used for building resilient structures.

• **Chilean eucalyptus.** *Eucaliptus*
This wood is very similar to eucalyptus (very hard, dense, light, strong, fine textured and durable), but with a darker reddish color.

• **Ash.** *Fraxinus excelsior*
This wood is quite hard and dense, with a yellowish color and very beautiful grain. It is very flexible and difficult to work, and it does not stain well. It is commonly used in wood turning.

• **Mottled ash.** *Fraxinus excelsior*
This wood has the characteristic knot pattern of wood from the root of the tree. It is cut into sheets that are used for marquetry work and veneering.

• **Beech.** *Fagus sylvatica*
This yellowish wood is heavy and flexible, even-grained with few knots. It is very susceptible to insect attacks and is resistant to heat. Large quantities of this wood are used in manufacturing furniture, especially curved and shaped pieces.

• **Myrtle.** *Fagara heitzii*
This is a hard wood without knots that has a very light color similar to lemon. It is used exclusively for the interiors of furniture and decorative veneer.

• **Walnut.** *Juglans regia*
This wood is dark brown, hard, compact, dense, and fine-grained, with straight or wavy grain. The wavy grain is characteristically dark. Susceptible to insect attacks, it is easily worked and polished. It is used for carving, furniture, veneering, and marquetry.

• **American walnut.** *Juglans nigra*
A dark brown to reddish black hardwood that is darker than European walnut. It has a rough texture and straight grain. It is used for making furniture, carving, and veneering.

• **Olive.** *Olea europea*
A hard, compact wood, with a yellowish color and dark grain. It is ideal for turning and finishing. Has a characteristic odor. It is used for wood-turning projects.

Mottled ash.

Beech.

Myrtle.

Walnut.

American walnut.

Olive.

Elm.

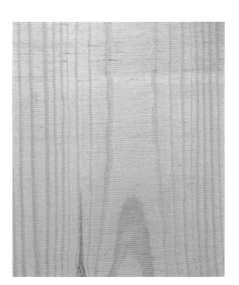

Palisander.

Pearwood.

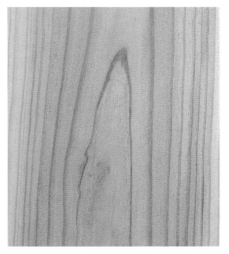

Norway spruce.

Galician pine.

Yellow pine.

• **Elm.** *Ulmus* spp.
A dark red wood with a coarse grain that is quite hard. Resistant to wear, humidity, and insects. It is difficult to finish.

• **Palisander.** *Machaerium* spp.
Dalbergia spp.
This name is used for a great many species of different tropical trees of the genera *Machaerium* and *Dalbergia*, whose colors range from dark red to violet brown or almost black, some with fine pronounced grain and others with large grain. These trees are compact with hard uniform fibers and are used for making high-quality furniture. They are also known as Palo Santo and jacaranda. The various species of palisander are in danger of extinction.

• **Pearwood.** *Pirus comunis*
A pinkish brown hardwood with a fine, dense grain, and uniform rings that are barely visible. It is resistant to insect attack. Easy to work and finish.

• **Norway spruce.** *Picea abies*
A yellowish white wood that is soft and resinous. The dark grain has a sienna-ochre color and is straight and even. It is used in carpentry and for making the framework of furniture.

• **Galician pine.** *Pinus pinaster*
This wood is resinous, soft, light, and not very dense, with a pinkish or yellowish white color. It is elastic, stable, and easy to work. It is used for making furniture and covering veneer.

• **Yellow pine.** *Pinus palustris*
A very resinous, softwood that has a yellowish red color with a characteristic straight and even reddish grain. Now it is used for making furniture, but in the past it was used for making doors, windows, and beams.

• **Oregon pine.** *Pseudotsuga douglas*
A soft, resinous wood, that has a darker color than other species of pine and an even grain. It is mainly used for doing decorative carpentry and for making molding.

• **Plantain.** *Platanus orientalis.*
Platanus ecerifolia
This wood is somewhat hard, flexible, and heavy, and dark yellow in color with pronounced iridescence. It is susceptible to insect attack. It is similar to beech and is used in wood turning, for veneer coverings and in furniture manufacturing.

• **Oak.** *Quercus robur*
Oak is a high-quality, hard, compact wood with an earthy yellow color and straight fibers. Depending on how it is cut, it can show a very characteristic wide grain. It is resistant to humidity. It is used in exterior carpentry and for making furniture and flooring.

• **Oak burl.** *Quercus robur*
An earthy-colored wood showing a characteristic knot pattern. It is cut in sheets from the roots of the tree for use as veneer.

• **Sapele mahogany.** *Entandrophragma cylindricum*
This wood is somewhat soft, semidense, and aromatic, with a smooth texture and a gray-pink color with strong iridescent highlights. It is easy to work and varnish. It is used for making furniture and doing veneer work.

• **Teak.** *Tectona grandis*
A very hard, dense wood that is stable and fine-grained with a dark red color. It is very resistant to wear. Used for indoor and outdoor furniture, in wood turning and veneering. This species is in danger of extinction.

Oregon pine.

Plantain.

Oak.

Oak burl.

Sapele mahogany.

Teak.

Wood parts and pieces

Whether restoring an entire piece of furniture, or making minor changes like adding or replacing some of its pieces, it is practical to use standard-sized parts that are commercially available. Therefore it is important to be familiar with the different shapes and sizes of these parts and pieces. Many shapes can be divided into groups: wood cut into different shapes without any further manipulation (boards and sheets), manufactured parts (dowels, sticks, molding, and appliques), and fabricated sheets (chipboard, plywood, and medium-density fiberboard). It is also possible to buy pieces made of different types of wood (depending on the design and species), made of two different materials (medium-density molding faced with wood or premade sheets of marquetry), or previously treated for a specific use (bleached or stained sheets or boards that have been treated for exterior use).

It is a good idea to save parts and leftover pieces of the sizes and shapes used, because they may be useful for other projects. It is also recommended to save pieces of wood, molding, legs, and

Boards (A) and veneer (B).

so on from old furniture pieces for future restorations or renovations.

Boards

Wood pieces cut directly from the tree are generically called boards. They are long straight pieces with rectangular sections that range from 8 to 20 feet (2.5 to 6.5 m) long, 2 to 4 inches (5 to 10 cm) thick, and 6 to 10 inches (15 to 25 cm) wide. It is possible to find parts of other sizes and shapes on the market depending on the demand.

Veneer and inlay wood

• Veneer
Very thin wood sheets measuring from $\frac{1}{32}$ to $\frac{1}{24}$ inch (0.8 to 5 mm) in thickness that are used for veneering and marquetry work are called veneer. The

different looks and grain patterns depend on the part of the tree from which the wood is taken and on the way it is cut. The veneer can be any of the following: *smooth* (regular grain), *wavy* (varied grain and tones that look like waves), *watery* (with sinuous waves producing a moire effect), *birdseye* (with small very closely spaced knots), *burl* (with knots surrounded by a large number of rings), *crotch* (with irregular markings and accentuated coloring), or *mottle figured* (with sinuous graining and contrasting figures).

• Inlay wood
Inlay wood comes in various sizes with a thickness ranging from $\frac{5}{32}$ to $\frac{3}{8}$ inches (4 to 10 mm) and is used for inlay work. The most commonly used pieces are of medium thickness, about $\frac{3}{16}$ inches (5 mm).

Different species of wood veneers.

Boards of various sizes and shapes.

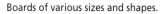

Manufactured shapes

• Dowels

These are rod-shaped pieces of various diameters that are used for reinforcing joints between two pieces of wood. The most useful are the grooved ones because they offer a larger surface for applying glue, so they adhere better than smooth dowels.

• Strips

These are pieces with a rectangular section ranging from $\frac{7}{16}$ to $\frac{3}{4}$ inches by $\frac{3}{4}$ to $1\frac{1}{2}$ inches (1 to 2 cm by 2 to 4 cm) wide and of varying lengths. Strips with quarter-round and half-round profiles are also available. They have many uses, among them holding glass in windows or panels in doors.

• Legs

These are the pieces that hold furniture up off the floor. There is a wide variety of legs on the market, made of different woods and in different styles.

• Molding

These decorative strips with relief and a carved profile are used for decorating furniture. There is a large selection of moldings on the market, most of them mass produced, but some that are handmade. Normally, they must be purchased in standard lengths determined by the manufacturers (6 to 12 feet [2 to 4 m]) but some stores will sell them cut to order if there is enough demand.

Various molding designs.

• Balustrades

These are a type of column that are usually turned on a lathe and decorated with molding or other motifs. The larger ones are used for making railings, while the smaller ones are used as decorative elements on furniture.

• Appliques

These carved pieces of wood come in many different sizes and are applied to the surface of the wood as decoration.

• Pulls and finials

Pulls are attached to the fronts of drawers and doors on furniture so they can be opened and closed. There are different types of wood pulls commercially available, including unfinished, stained, and varnished.

Finials are turned or carved pieces that are placed high up at the edge or on the top of a piece of furniture, purely for aesthetic reasons.

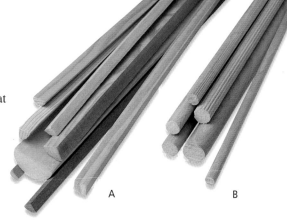

Strips (A) and dowels (B).

Various types of carved appliques.

Two types of legs.

Different models of pulls.

Different types of finials.

Commercial marquetry pieces

• Inlay borders

These small strips with a rectangular section are mainly used for inlay work. There are solid wood strips made of boxwood or other woods, which are stained to imitate ebony. There are also marquetry strips, which are usually wider than the solid wood strips, that are made of different kinds of natural-colored or stained wood, in the form of geometric compositions.

• Decorative inlay pieces

It is possible to purchase pieces of marquetry that are already assembled and ready to apply. Just like the strips, they can be made of solid wood (the most simple and affordable) or with different types of wood (more elaborate and costly).

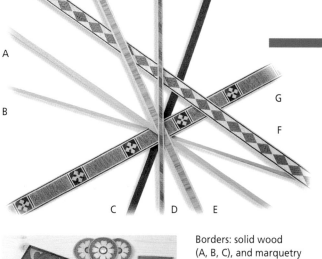

Borders: solid wood (A, B, C), and marquetry (D, E, F, G).

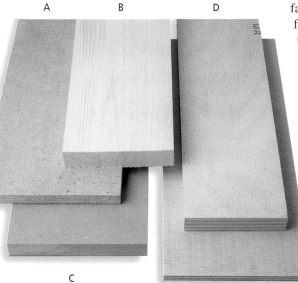

Pieces of decorative marquetry.

Manufactured boards

• Solid wood

These boards are made from several strips or pieces of solid wood that are glued and joined together at the edges.

• Plywood

These boards are made from sheets of wood that are glued one over the other, with the grain aligned in different directions. An odd number of sheets are glued to each other, turning the direction of the fiber or the grain of alternating sheets at right angles to each other. This makes a board that is stable and resistant to warping. The boards are classified according to the quality of the outside surfaces: Class A is for boards whose faces are clear and have no imperfections. Class B includes those that have some imperfections, such as small knots or stains. Finally, class C is made up of those whose faces have large knots or cracks. The sizes of the boards range from $\frac{1}{8}$ to 1 inch (3 to 25 mm) thick, and are 8 feet long by 4 feet wide (2.4 by 1.2 m).

• Chipboard

These boards are made by gluing chips and splinters of wood with synthetic resins and pressing them at high temperatures. Different types of manufactured boards are available, depending on the shape and the size of the wood particles, their distribution, and the type of resins used as adhesives. These kinds of boards are more stable than plywood and do not have defects like solid wood. Their dimensions can be as great as 6 feet wide by 24 feet long (2 by 8 m), which is an advantage in large-scale projects.

• Fiberboard

This material is made of wood that has been reduced to fibers that have been glued together with synthetic resins in a high-frequency press, resulting in a reconstituted wood product. Boards of different densities can be manufactured depending on the pressure and the resins that are used: high density, low density, and medium density. The medium-density fiberboard is made by joining dry wood fibers with synthetic resins, resulting in a uniform structure with a fine texture and a perfect finish on the faces and the edges. It is used in place of wood and is worked in the same manner. Medium-density fiberboard is manufactured in thicknesses that range from $\frac{1}{4}$ to $1\frac{1}{4}$ inches (6 to 32 mm), the most widely used being 4 feet wide by 8 feet long (1.2 by 2.4 m).

Chipboard (A), solid wood board (B), medium-density fiberboard (C), and plywood (D).

Main problems of wood and their detection

Wood is an organic material, which can naturally undergo changes if the environmental conditions vary. The factors that can cause changes are humidity, temperature, and exposure to light. These three factors, in themselves damaging, can encourage the appearance and proliferation of other problems such as insects and mildew.

Insects

Insects are responsible for the worst and most extensive effects of damage to wood, even to the point of destroying it completely. Xylophagous insects (*xilos* = wood; *fago* = eater) not only consume wood but also live, develop, and reproduce in it. Their life cycle has four phases: egg, larva, pupa, and adult. These insects reach the first stage after going through several mutations.

Insects are not able to regulate their body temperature. Their growth, maturation, and reproduction all take place at a certain temperature, 77°F (25°C), and slow down as the temperature decreases from 77° to 59°F (25° to 15°C).

In order to realize the serious problem that insects can represent, it is necessary to understand the way in which they attack. The problem may even be more serious if we keep in mind that the hole that indicates their presence is a sign of an adult that may have gone on to colonize other wood objects and structures. The female lays her eggs in any split, crack, or hole in the wood. Weeks later the larva emerges and immediately bores into the wood, where it will live and bore numerous tunnels until its adult phase.

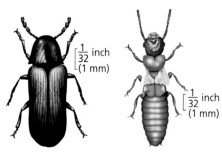

Example of the adult wood beetle.

Termite

Different species of insects can attack wood. They vary according to country and climate. The most common are termites and wood beetles. The wood beetle finds ideal conditions for its development in countries with a mild climate. It leaves a characteristic trail, similar to sawdust or wood powder, near the exit hole that the adult has made. Termites are social insects that live in colonies. They thrive in dry wood as well as in wet wood, and even some subterranean species exist.

It is important to remember that insects do not attack manufactured boards (plywood, chipboard, and fiberboard), because the adhesives and resins that are used in their production and in their coatings are poisonous to them.

An example of termite damage. The inside of the wood is completely destroyed, whereas the outside looks almost perfect.

Mildew

The greater the humidity in a piece of wood the more likely it is to be attacked by mildew. It can grow on the surface or in the cracks and openings of wood that is not well preserved, that is very wet, that is not well ventilated, or that has contact with the ground. Some kinds of mildew can cause from small to rather extended surface staining, whereas others can destroy a large part of the surface of an object.

An example of mildew attacking the surface of an object made of wicker.

The effects of light and changes in humidity and temperature

The damaging effects of light are directly proportional to the length of time of exposure and, furthermore are cumulative. The most damaging source of light is the sun.

Sudden changes in humidity and temperature (two factors that always go hand-in-hand), can cause the wood to move. The effects of these changes will be greater when the wood is thin. Veneer and panels can move, curl, and break in a very short time, whereas a board can take several hours to warp. These three factors combined can cause serious deterioration in the wood and can encourage attack from mildew and insects.

Solutions and treatments

We have shown that there are many factors that cause wood to deteriorate and that the resulting problems are also varied. The best solution, without a doubt, is prevention. The conservation of wood furniture, objects, and structural elements must necessarily be based on preventing, localizing, and quickly solving the problems. The pictures and text below explain the steps that should be taken. Restoring or repairing a wood object is of no use if it is then exposed to detrimental factors. To eliminate insect problems, which are certainly the worst, the wood must be thoroughly disinfected.

Disinfection

The purpose of disinfection is to totally eliminate all wood-boring insects in all phases of their life cycle. There are several methods, some of which can only be carried out in laboratories or by specialized companies.

The simplest method is based on the application of toxic substances (poisons) in liquid or gas form. However, keep in mind that these toxic substances, depending on their composition and concentration, can affect the environment and the people living in the house. Therefore, it is of utmost importance to wear protective equipment such as latex gloves and a respirator. Also, the disinfectant should be applied outdoors or in a well-ventilated area, and any leftover chemicals should not be disposed of in the natural environment.

Liquid insecticides are mixed with solvents to help them penetrate the wood to combat wood borers. Their success depends on the efficient delivery of the product to all the areas that have been attacked. Their effect is curative (killing the insects) and preventive (if the wood has been completely impregnated, they can work for quite some time or prevent new attacks).

Paradichlorobenzine is an active ingredient in the formula for mothballs and tablets. It is a solid, but the fumes that emanate from it produce the effect. If used alone and in high concentrations, it can become toxic to humans. It stops working when the application is discontinued, so its effect is only curative.

The best system combines both curative and preventive effects—that is to say, the use of a disinfectant liquid together with a gas.

1- The first step before disinfecting any object is to clean all surfaces to ensure that the liquid disinfectant does not adhere and fix the grime to the wood. Any dust left on the wood can be eliminated by wiping the surface with a cloth. Special attention is paid to areas that have corners and gaps (where crosspieces attach to the top, joints, where boards come together, and so on) and areas that are difficult to reach (inside and under a piece of furniture, drawers, and so on). Dust can be removed with a small brush.

2- Latex gloves and a respirator should be put on for protection before attempting to work with liquid disinfectants. First, the liquid is injected into every hole in the wood with a syringe so the disinfectant can penetrate the wood, following the tunnels that the insects made when leaving the wood.

3- After the disinfectant is injected, several coats of it are applied using a wide brush. Every surface of the object must be completely covered.

4- Next, a disinfecting bag is made. A sheet of heavy polyethylene plastic is cut according to the size of the object that is to be wrapped. The object is placed on the center of the plastic sheet and the sides wrapped, attaching them with plastic packing tape, making sure that no openings are left. One side is left open. The plastic is wrapped so that the bag has the smallest volume possible.

5- Several commercial moth pellets are placed inside the bag. The number needed depends on the volume of the bag: the larger the volume, the greater the number of pellets. Three pellets are suggested for an object or furniture piece that is small to medium in size. If the moth pellets are individually wrapped, it will be necessary to make small holes in their packaging by repeatedly poking them with a needle.

6- The success of the disinfecting process depends on the creation of a highly toxic atmosphere that will kill all insects. It is a good idea to leave a minimal amount of air in the bag to help create this atmosphere. A household vacuum cleaner set on low is a very practical system for extracting air from the bag. The opening in the bag should be sealed quickly with packing tape.

7· Finally, the date the bag was prepared is noted on a piece of paper or cardboard and attached to the top of the plastic. The bag is left in place for 15 days, which is the amount of time considered necessary to kill all the insects.

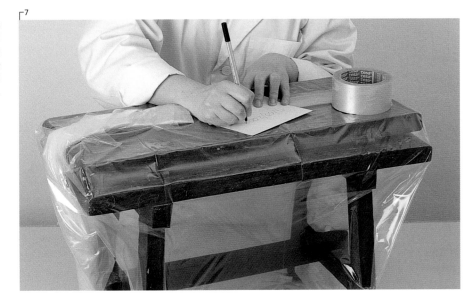

7

ADVICE FOR CONSERVING WOOD		
Factors and Problems	**Consequences**	**Prevention**
• Humidity and temperature (in excess or sudden changes)	• Warping, cracking, and breaking of the wood. The thinner the wood the faster this will happen. • Possible chemical reactions. • Damage of wax- and varnish-based finishes, resulting in a whitish, opaque coating. • Encourage attack by insects and mildew.	• Remove objects from sources of heat, such as radiators. • Remove objects from humid areas or near water. • Protect wood with the appropriate finish (varnish, wax, and so on) and regularly check its condition. • Regularly and thoroughly clean objects, including the back and underside. • Periodically inspect the piece.
• Light	• Changes in the color of the wood, which will either lighten or darken. • Increase in the surface temperature of the wood. • Damage of wax- and varnish-based finishes. • May encourage attack by insects and mildew.	• Remove objects from sources of intense light, such as windows that let in too much light or powerful lamps. • Install cotton or linen curtains over openings that let in sunlight.
• Mildew	• Stains on the wood. • Destruction of parts of the wood.	• Put the object in a dry and ventilated place. • Avoid letting wood come in direct contact with the ground.
• Insects	• Holes in the surface and tunnels in the wood. • Total destruction of objects and structural elements.	• Apply a finish or refinish the wood, and check its condition regularly. • Cover the holes and cracks on the surface of the wood. • Regularly clean all surfaces of the object, including the underside, the inside, and the back. • Periodically inspect for possible holes, telltale sawdust, and flying insects. • Avoid putting infested objects in contact with others that are free from insects.

c h a p t e r

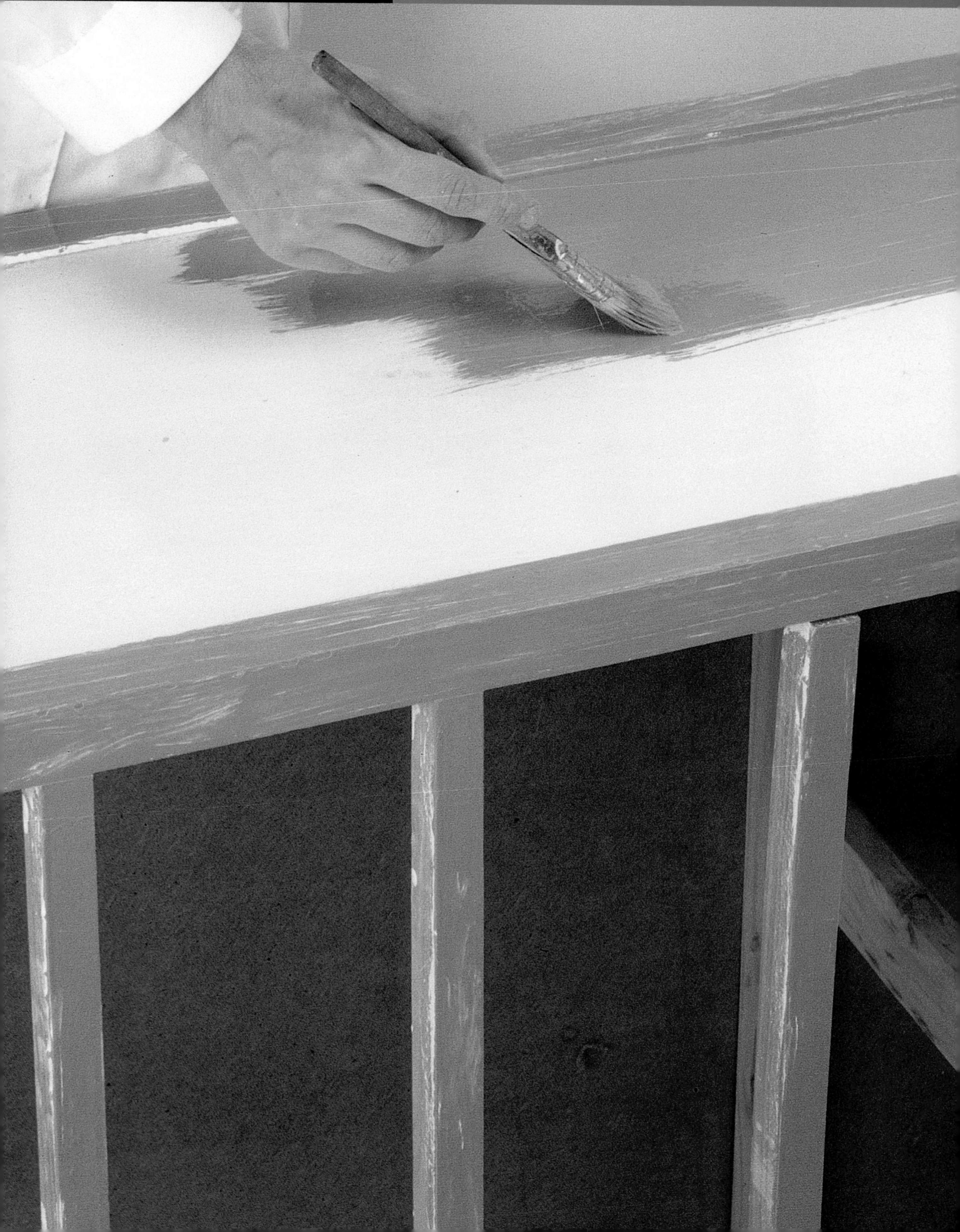

3 Processes

All restoration and renovation
projects require innumerable processes,
which vary depending on the condition and type of
furniture or object being repaired. In this chapter we show the
most common processes for solving potential problems. They are
grouped according to the order in which the steps should be
performed: establishing the condition of the piece, treating
the structure, adding and repairing parts, and refinishing
surfaces. To find the most appropriate solution for
any project, the reader can choose from the processes described in this chapter or from
those covered in the chapters on restoration and renovation.

Starting out

Before a restoration or renovation project is started, the general condition of the piece must be assessed. This way the amount of time needed for the project can be estimated, and decisions regarding the processes, materials, and tools that will be required can be made. If restoration is the goal, a detailed diagnosis of the problems is necessary after the general assessment. If renovation is chosen, a plan is made specifying the solutions to be applied, among them, the parts to be eliminated or added.

Diagnosis

The piece of furniture or object should be examined from all angles when making the diagnosis. It should be turned over, and drawers and shelves should be pulled out. Its general condition should be carefully noted, and then its characteristics and the condition of its parts should be listed in order. The carpentry work that is required, the condition of the wood, the type of object or furniture piece in question, and the condition of the accessories should all be evaluated. All this will aid the restoration process and help retain as many of the original elements as possible. Substitutions should only be made when proper use or function is affected or when areas of inlay or marquetry are missing.

A bedside table: diagnosis of its general condition

This bedside table is constructed of pine wood and veneered in sapele mahogany. The piece will be given a tinted, shellac finish.

The structure is generally in good condition. No parts are loose, and no major breaks are observed, so reinforcement will not be necessary. The drawer is in good shape and slides perfectly. The finish coat is in poor condition: It is stained and scratched, and it has some opaque areas. It will be removed and lacquered again.

Checking the condition of the parts

The furniture piece is turned over and the undersides and hidden areas are examined.

The veneer that covers the frame is partially missing from the lower ends of the legs. New veneer will have to be applied. A veneer with similar characteristics to the existing one must be found and stained to match.

It is also noted that one of the moldings of the center shelf is about to come off, and its end is broken. The existing molding will have to be attached with nails and a similar one found to repair the missing part. It will later be stained.

Project

Several things must be kept in mind when performing a renovation. First, the furniture or object must be examined to establish its general condition. Then all parts must be inspected to determine which ones can be saved, which ones need to be repaired, and which ones have to be replaced. Next, a sketch or drawing of the object is made indicating the colors, the pieces that need to be added or eliminated, the finishes, and so on. The sketch can be made to scale and very elaborate, or it can be a simple drawing where the most important points are indicated. In either case, it will serve as a guide for the project.

Renovating a small table

A small table made from solid pine. Its structure is in very good condition.

1- The surface of the table is stained and has several scratches and dents resulting from years of use. The best solution is to apply a painted finish.

2- The characteristics of the table are noted. Then, all of the parts are measured and a drawing of it is made. In this case, the sketch is being made to scale. It is a good idea to draw a perspective view first. If necessary, views of the different sides can also be drawn.

3- The solutions that are going to be implemented can be shown on the drawing. The colors can be chosen using a color fan and different samples of inks and paint on wood. The drawing can be colored to show how the project will look when it is finished. This way a decision can be made about whether it is necessary to change a color or to opt for a different finish. Then the pieces that are to be added are drawn, in this case, drawer pulls, whose function will be decorative.

The structure

The structure is the most important part of any piece of furniture. It is the constructive element that holds the whole piece together. Any intervention here should be minimal, because any change or modification could require the use of complicated techniques and processes that require a certain amount of experience. The most common processes are dismantling and reassembling, protecting the parts, and gluing and reinforcing pieces.

Disassembly

It may be necessary to disassemble a piece of furniture completely. All of the steps must be carried out with great care, to avoid scratching or breaking the wood and losing nails, screws, and other decorative elements. The process should always take place in a large space, where the parts can be dismantled in order and properly marked and stored. If the piece in question has a complicated structure, the placement of each part is noted, and the steps taken referenced. Marking or numbering the parts will later help guide the assembly process, allowing the tasks to be performed faster and more efficiently.

Disassembling a dresser

The disassembly of a dresser begins by removing the drawers. The more complicated parts should follow, such as the marble that covers the top of the dresser.

1- Before taking out the drawers completely, each one should be consecutively numbered and labeled with a sticker. To indicate the location of each drawer, a sticker is placed on the inside of the dresser bearing the same number as the drawer.

2- Next, one drawer is placed on a large work surface. The screwdriver is held in a vertical position to remove the screws from the drawer pulls and the keyhole on the front of the drawer, while care is taken not to damage the wood.

3- The parts are stored in a plastic container with separations to keep them from getting mixed up. Finally, the container is marked with the same number as the drawer. The parts can also be stored wrapped in small paper packages or placed in several bags.

Removing hardware and hinges

The removal of hardware—whether keyholes, hinges, or decorative elements—requires the removal of the nails or screws that hold them to the wood.

1- In this example, the keyhole is firmly attached to the wood with nails. The head of the nail is grasped with pincers and pulled firmly. The nail is very old and offers resistance. The best approach is to make a slight rocking motion while pulling. A thin piece of wood is placed under the head of the pincers to prevent the wood from becoming damaged.

2- Any tool may be used as a lever to lift hinges or other hardware from the surface of the wood. Here the keyhole is pried up by inserting the end of a screwdriver between the metal and the wood. A thin piece of wood is used to protect the surface of the furniture from scratches.

3- A screwdriver is held vertically, and some pressure is applied while removing the screws. If the screws offer resistance, the end of the screwdriver handle is tapped with a hammer to loosen them.

Protecting parts

In some restoration and renovation projects, it is not possible to disassemble all parts, either because they are fragile or because the process is complicated. In such cases, these elements should be carefully protected against breakage and damage from the chemicals used in treating the wood.

Protecting seats and glass pieces

Seats made of cane or rush are very delicate by nature, and it is important to protect them if harsh chemicals are used. Glass and mirrors need extra protection because they are fragile.

Masking tape should be carefully applied around the edges to protect any kind of glass, like this antique mirror. Then a piece of heavy paper or plastic is cut to the approximate size of the area that is to be covered. It is held with masking tape to the tape that was previously applied around the edges.

To protect elements made of cane, reed, or any other delicate material, a fairly wide masking tape should be used. The perimeter of the caned seat is covered by applying the tape carefully, leaving no open areas.

Filling and gluing

One problem that is common to most pieces of furniture and objects is a fragile and unstable structure. This is usually due to broken parts (such as panels, tops, and legs) or to the separation of pieces at the joints of the structure. In either case, the solutions are simple and do not require complicated processes.

Repairing with commercial fillers

Commercial fillers are very practical for repairing tabletops or the surfaces of other wood pieces that have been attacked by insects. This type of filler, which is ready to use, is available in various colors and textures.

Filler is forced into each hole with a metal spatula, and left to dry. Then, it is smoothed by sanding with fine 180-grit sandpaper.

Preparing a filler

Filler can be made by mixing fine sawdust with carpenter's glue (PVA), plaster of Paris, and tap water until a thick, smooth paste is created. It is perfect for applying to any crack in the wood.

1- The sawdust adds a texture similar to that of wood, the glue holds the components together, and the plaster, when dry, adds hardness to the mixture.

2- When repairing a crack in a shelf from inside a piece of furniture, filler is pressed into the crack with a metal spatula until the space between the two sides of the board is filled. It is then left to dry for 24 hours.

3- Later, the surface of the filler is smoothed with a piece of 180-grit sandpaper, following the direction of the grain. Both sides of the board are sanded until the two surfaces are smooth and level.

Preparing hot glues

Rabbit skin glue, applied hot, is the most appropriate adhesive for repairing small decorative elements and attaching pieces of marquetry. For gluing together parts of furniture, structural pieces that support weight, or very large pieces, a stronger mixture can be used. Both glues are prepared in a similar manner.

1- To make rabbit skin glue (A), place one part rabbit skin glue granules and two parts tap water in a glass jar. Next, let it sit for 24 hours so the mixture can soften. To make a stronger mixture (B), put one part granulated *bone glue* in a jar and add the same amount of water. Let this sit for 24 hours also.

2- Both types of glue are prepared by heating in a double boiler. Place the jar with the softened glue into a pot of water, and warm it on a hot plate. The action of the hot water will cause the glue to slowly dissolve and acquire a liquid consistency. Do not let it heat any more because it will lose its adhesive power.

Gluing techniques

There are many different techniques and tools for applying adhesives and for holding parts when gluing together structures of a certain complexity.

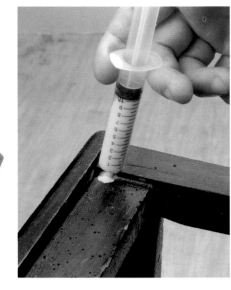

Syringes are most useful for applying glue in areas that are very difficult to reach with a brush. In this case, glue is applied to a chair's defective joint in a small space between the seat rail and the front leg.

A belt clamp is the most appropriate tool for joining right angles. It is used here to hold together the frame of a chair with square legs and seat rails at right angles.

Bar clamps are useful for joining new pieces to the existing wood and properly gluing joints that are next to each other. It is a good idea to place protective blocks between the object and the clamps.

The tourniquet method is ideal for holding objects that are not parallel or that are curved. This system is most commonly used for chairs because of their complex construction. The tourniquet allows complicated joints to be glued quickly and easily. Force is applied by twisting the cord around a piece of wood. In this case, the tourniquet is holding the legs of the chair to the back.

Gluing curved parts

Clamps are inadequate for repairing tabletops and flat pieces with curved edges, because they are difficult to hold and tend to slip and move.

When bonding pieces of this type, glue is applied before mounting them to a board (chipboard in this case) with nails used as stops. They are placed in such a way that as much pressure as possible will be applied to the glued area. The carpenter's glue is allowed to dry for 24 hours, and later the nails are removed.

Assembly

The final assembly is carried out when the restoration or renovation is finished. This process affects the structure of the piece directly, so it is covered in this section and not in the finishing sections.

Assembly is always more complicated than disassembly. Correct assembly of each part will greatly depend on the instructions and notes made during disassembly, as well as on the careful storage and numbering of the parts. Keep in mind that how well the piece is assembled will affect the solidity of the piece as well as its overall look and future use. Incorrect assembly will affect the structure and cause poorly fitting joints and breaking of some parts.

Assembling an extendable table

After finishing the restoration process, it is time to assemble an extendable table made of solid mahogany. Every assembly project is different, depending on the type of furniture or object, its quality, and its intended use. However, the goal in every case is to make a strong, solid structure.

1- Here, the table legs have wheels that are in poor condition; they are completely worn out and broken in some places, so they will have to be replaced. A few drops of oil are applied at the point where the wheels meet the legs.

2- Each wheel is removed by pulling firmly. If the wheels offer resistance, some more oil may be added, and then a pair of pliers can be used for pulling them out.

3- The tabletop is placed face down on a large surface, in this case on the floor. All parts are gathered and put where they belong to make certain that nothing is missing. Next, the connectors, the screws, the washers, and the tools needed for assembly are prepared.

4- Glue is applied to the rails that connect the legs. A wide flat brush is used to apply carpenter's glue (PVA) on the tenon of the rail.

5- The rail is attached to the leg by inserting the tenon into the mortise. A mallet with a nylon head can be used to strike the free end of the rail softly until it is set inside the leg.

6- The rails and the legs are attached at their original locations, making sure they fit well. The four rails are mounted to the tabletop using their original screws. The original screws are also used to attach the inside rails that function as the extension mechanism.

7- Once they have been attached, a try square is used to check if the legs are properly mounted. They should form a perfect right angle with respect to the rails and the tabletop.

└8

8- Next, the old wheels are replaced by new ones. The new wheels have a smaller diameter rod where they attach to the legs. To solve this problem, a piece is added that will hold the new wheel in place. A hole is bored in the center of a dowel with a rotary tool fitted with a small drill bit. The dowel should be the same diameter as the hole in the leg where the old wheels will be inserted.

┌6

┌7

┌9

┌10

┌11

9- The dowels are inserted into the holes in each leg, making sure they fit snugly.

10- The wheels are then attached to the turned legs with screws. The newly purchased wheels are different from the old ones. The new ones are slightly larger, and each one can support up to 55 pounds (25 kg). After the wheels have been replaced, 24 hours should elapse before the table is moved.

11- The shiny metal on the four wheels contrasts with the mahogany's shellac finish. The surface of the metal can be darkened to match the surface of the table. A coat of undiluted asphalt is applied using a soft, medium-sized brush.

┌12

12- The restored and assembled table has a solid and resistant structure. It can be placed in the dining room for daily use.

Parts

The overall look of a piece of furniture largely depends on the finish and the parts and accessories that make up the piece. Adding or replacing some parts can completely change an object, making it look very different from the original. However, if the piece has a problem that affects its structure, it may be necessary to replace the parts that are broken or beyond repair.

Replacing parts

This approach is used almost exclusively in furniture renovation projects. Molding can be used to decorate the corners of panels and drawers or to frame design motifs. Pulls, knobs, and rings can also play a merely decorative function because they change the look of a door or drawer. The radical transformation of a piece of furniture, which can give it new use, may require that doors, covers, or lids be removed.

1- Lids: A lid can be added to a small drawer to turn it into a jewelry box. A piece of thin plywood is cut to fit over the drawer. Hinges should then be aligned on the inside of the lid and the placement of the screws marked with a gimlet. The step is repeated on one of the edges of the box. The placement is measured, centered, and marked to attach the hinges over the edge of one side of the box.

2- Next, the screws are inserted through the hinges into the lid, making sure that they close perfectly.

Adding pulls and lids

The overall look of a furniture piece can be changed by adding certain elements, such as molding, doors and lids, pulls, rings.

Pulls: The pull is centered on the panel or board where it will be attached. The exact location is marked on the wood by tracing its outline using a pencil with soft lead. The pencil or a gimlet can be used to make a small hole at the location where the screw will be inserted. The pull is placed on the mark, and the screws are inserted into the holes. Small nails or screws can be used to attach it.

¹

²

Adding molding

A fast and simple way to change the look of a dresser is to add decorative molding to the drawers. The first step is measuring the side of the drawer.

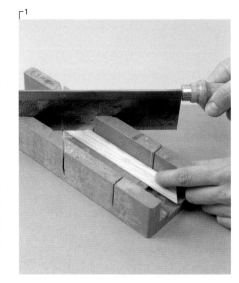

1- An attractive piece of molding is purchased from a store. The measurement taken from the drawer is marked on the piece, indicating where the cut will be made. Then the molding is placed in a miter box and held against the side with one hand, while the miter saw is inserted into the guides and the desired angle is cut at the pencil mark.

2- Carpenter's glue is applied to the back of the molding with a small brush, and it is then carefully put in place on the edge of the drawer. It is nailed with two brads to ensure a good bond between the piece and the drawer front. The process is repeated on all of the drawers.

Replacing pieces

Replacing existing pieces is more complicated than adding or removing elements. In restoration projects, as many parts as possible should be preserved; they should be replaced only when the function of the furniture or object is affected. In renovations, it is not necessary to save all the original elements, so they are replaced or removed based on practical concerns.

Replacing a drawer guide

Drawers tend to break easily from constant use. Following is a complete explanation of how to repair them.

1- One of the guides of this drawer is worn out from continual use and excess weight in the drawer.

2- The process begins by leveling the broken guide. The section that will have to be removed to level the surface of the guide is measured and marked.

3- The wood is removed up to the mark with a metal plane. Then the side is leveled and smoothed with a rasp.

4- A piece of solid wood board, similar in width to the sides of the drawer, is cut to size. Carpenter's glue (PVA) is applied to the area being repaired, and the new wood piece is set on it and held in place with a clamp at each end.

5- After waiting 24 hours, the clamps are removed. Then the extra material is removed with the plane until the new guide is the same height as the one on the other side of the drawer.

Surfaces

Finishing a wood surface requires diverse and elaborate processes. Because the outcome of any project depends on its exterior finish, no restoration or renovation can be considered complete until the various parts have been properly cleaned, the wood has been prepared, and the piece has received the final protective coat. The different finishes help protect and enhance the wood.

Stripping

In both restoration and renovation projects, is necessary to strip the wood. Pieces that may require stripping include those with a thick coat of paint covering a high-quality wood, with large areas of discoloration due to heavy use, or with a dark-colored varnish that now will be replaced by a more natural color. The different ways of stripping wood can be grouped by system: mechanical (sanding and hot air gun) and chemical (alcohol, caustic soda, and stripping agents).

Stripping with alcohol

Alcohol is a useful stripping agent for two reasons: It is nontoxic, and it is inexpensive. Alcohol is used to help remove shellac finishes.

A generous amount of alcohol is applied to an area of the wood, in this case a tabletop, with a wide brush. It is left on a while to soften the surface coat, which is then removed by scrubbing with a number 000 steel wool pad. Finally, the wood is wiped with a cotton cloth or strands soaked with alcohol.

In a bucket of hot water, 2.2 pounds (1 kg) of caustic soda are diluted in 5 quarts plus 6 ounces (5 L) of water, if the layer of paint is not very thick, or in 2 quarts (2 L) of water if it is. The mixture is stirred until the caustic soda dissolves completely. In this example, a drawer covered with several layers of latex paint is being stripped. The caustic soda is applied with a cotton cloth and scrubbed in the direction of the grain of the wood until the paint is removed. Then the wood is rinsed using a cloth saturated with water.

Stripping with caustic soda

Caustic soda in solution is used solely for stripping solid pine, because it is the only wood that can stand up to such an aggressive product. Because caustic soda is a chemical irritant, it is necessary to use long neoprene gloves, a respirator, safety glasses, and heavy cotton clothing.

Stripping with commercial gels

Commercial strippers are widely used. All of them, regardless of their consistency and form, are irritants and are toxic, so it is important to use neoprene gloves, a respirator, eye protection, and heavy cotton clothing when using them.

1- The first step consists of applying a gel stripper to the face of the drawer with a brush.

2- The gel is left for some time to soften the finish. Then, the paste is removed from the surface of the wood by scraping it off with a metal scraper and then wiping that on a piece of paper. It is finished by scrubbing the surface with a clean cotton rag soaked with paint thinner to remove any traces of the stripper.

Stripping with sandpaper

Manual sanding is the best way to remove thin coats of paint or varnish.

A power sander is ideal for smooth areas and large surfaces. The power sander can be used with different grades of sandpaper.

Sanders can be made to fit when stripping grooves and carved elements. A piece of sandpaper is rolled up to make a cylinder that will adapt to the width of the space that is to be sanded.

Sanding a surface with a piece of medium-grit sandpaper.

Sanding sponges are best for stripping curves and rounded areas. They adapt perfectly to the surface and sand it evenly.

Stripping with a hot air gun

The hot air gun is used for stripping solid wood with heavy coats of paint. Large areas can be cleaned with it in a relatively short time. It is useful for stripping doors and beams.

The action of the hot air causes the paint on the door to soften and blister. It is easily removed with a paint scraper. A hot air gun with air flow and temperature controls should be used to avoid burning the wood.

Cleaning

Before proceeding to finish the wood, it is important to thoroughly clean the exterior and interior of the furniture or object. Not doing so would diminish the quality of the work. Certain materials like marble and metal require special treatment.

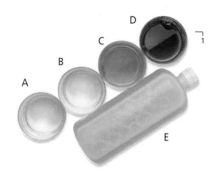

Preparing a reanimator

If the wood has not been treated in any way, the cleaning can be done with a reanimator, which will also impart depth and liveliness.

1- In a container, preferably glass or plastic with a measuring cap, $6\frac{3}{4}$ ounces (200 ml) of 96 percent alcohol (A), $6\frac{3}{4}$ ounces (200 ml) turpentine (B), $1\frac{3}{4}$ ounces (50 ml) plain vinegar (C), and $6\frac{3}{4}$ ounces (200 ml) linseed oil (D) are mixed. The bottle is closed tightly and shaken until the liquid is thoroughly mixed and turns cloudy (E).

2- The wood on this drawer is in good condition, but it has a surface coating that conceals its beauty. To improve its general appearance, a reanimator is applied with a piece of cotton, following the grain of the wood.

Cleaning marble

The first step in cleaning any type of marble consists of removing the dust from the surface.

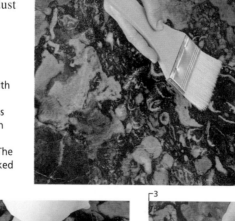

2- A solution consisting of 10 parts water with 1 part neutral soap (pH 7) and 4 drops of ammonia are mixed in a wide-mouthed glass jar. The mixture, which will thoroughly clean the marble without damaging it, is applied with a piece of cotton in a circular motion. The marble is then wiped with a cotton ball soaked with water and left to dry.

1- All dirt and dust on the surface should be wiped off using a wide brush with soft bristles to prevent the grime from getting into the pores of the marble.

3- The process is finished with the application of a transparent furniture wax to the surface of the marble with a cotton cloth. After the surface has completely dried, buff with a clean cotton cloth for a polished finish.

Cleaning metal

Metal hardware—such as pulls, hinges, locks, and keyholes—are found on most furniture and objects. Cleaning them requires specific processes that are very different from those used for wood or other types of materials.

1- In the case of bronze accessories, the piece (a handle) is wetted with alcohol to soften any surface grime.

2- Next, all surfaces of the handle are scrubbed with a wire brush until the layer of dirt darkening the metal is removed.

3- Then all surfaces are rubbed with a number 400 sandpaper until the metal is perfectly cleaned and polished.

4- The piece is buffed with a piece of number 000 steel wool, paying special attention to the grooves and corners.

5- A final coat of furniture wax is applied, making sure that all surfaces are covered to protect the bronze from tarnishing, especially the corners and grooves. In this case, the wax has a walnut-colored tint, which will darken the natural sheen of the clean, polished metal.

6- When dry, the surface of the handle is buffed using a brush with soft bristles until it acquires an even shine.

Cleaning interiors

The interiors of furniture and objects normally accumulate large amounts of dust and dirt. Any sawing, sanding, or planing done during restoration or renovation will increase that amount.

To clean the interiors of the cabinets, drawers, and shelves, it is best to use a household vacuum cleaner set on high. The dirt accumulated in the corners and angles can be removed with a wide brush and swept toward the vacuum hose.

Finishes

The different finishing processes are as important as any step carried out in restoration or renovation projects. The finish of any furniture piece or object will coat the wood, highlighting its qualities and protecting it from factors that can cause deterioration. There are many different finishes, all of which require the use of various materials and the application of more or less complicated techniques. Several of them are combinations or variations of the two most common finishes: wax and shellac. Commercial varnish products are easy to apply and guarantee the best results on stained or painted surfaces. Some light retouching will be necessary once the finish has been applied, to hide small flaws in the color.

Stains and paints are also considered finishes, because the former is applied to wood that has been previously prepared and the latter protects the surface.

Staining

The best way to stain a surface is to use a water-based dye, because it allows a uniform and homogenous application and because the tone can be darkened by adding more coats of color.

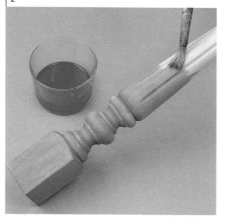

1- A water-based stain is prepared in a container by mixing hot water with water-soluble aniline powder. The amount of aniline can vary depending on the desired intensity of the color. The mixture should be tested on pieces of wood before the dye is applied.

2- A small brush is used to stain small surfaces and carved or turned pieces. Then the wood is left to dry completely. The water will raise the grain of the wood. This is smoothed by rubbing the surface with a piece of fine sandpaper in the direction of the grain.

Retouching

Retouching is done to hide small discolored areas on wood that has already been restored, either before the finish coat is applied or over the finish coat.

Two different methods can be used to hide small marks or scratches on the surface of the wood before the final coat is applied or even afterward. One consists of applying a stain directly to the discolored area using a fine retouching brush with soft hair.

Retouching markers of a color similar to that of the wood can also be used. The color is spread and evened out by tapping the retouched area with a finger until it is evenly blended over the surface of the wood.

Varnishing

Commercial varnishes are easy to use and, once dry, have a very durable finish; however, the wood must be sanded before they are applied.

Several kinds of varnishes are commercially available—including nitrocellulose filler, water-based varnish, and acrylic varnish—in different finishes (gloss, matte, or satin) and in different colors (wood tone or in bright colors). In this case, a table leg is being finished with a water-based varnish in a pastel pink color.

Preparing wax

Wax, the oldest finish, is applied directly to the wood, and once it has dried it is buffed with a wool or lint-free cotton cloth until it is glossy.

1- To make your own wax, use a hammer and chisel to cut $1\frac{3}{4}$ ounces (50 g) of paraffin, then weigh out $1\frac{3}{4}$ ounces (50 g) of pure beeswax and $1\frac{3}{4}$ ounces (50 g) of carnuba, which will add hardness to the wax.

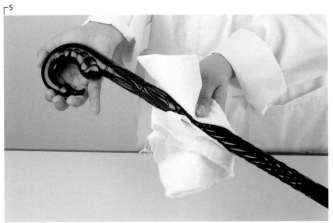

3- Remove the container, and let it cool slightly. While the mixture is still warm, add $8\frac{1}{2}$ ounces (250 ml) turpentine while stirring constantly. Finally, pour the wax into a wide-mouthed metal container. It is a good idea to use a container with a tight-fitting lid to keep the turpentine from evaporating.

4- The wax will become solid when it cools. A small amount of wax is placed on a cotton rag and a thin coat applied to the walking stick. Then it is left to dry.

5- The surface of the walking stick is then buffed with a clean cotton cloth.

2- Place the three ingredients into a metal container and heat it in a double boiler, stirring with a long stick or spatula until the liquid is thoroughly mixed.

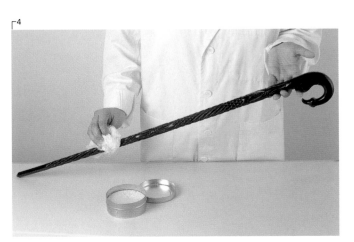

Preparing shellac

Although different types of ready-to-use liquid shellac are available, preparing shellac from scratch is a quick and easy process that requires little work and can be done by anyone.

1- First, weigh out $1\frac{3}{4}$ ounces (50 g) of pure shellac flakes.

2- Place them into a narrow-mouthed glass jar with a tight-fitting lid, which will keep the mixture from evaporating.

3- Add 16 ounces ($\frac{1}{2}$ L) of 96 percent alcohol, and close the jar. Wait until the shellac has completely dissolved. (Shaking the jar from time to time will help the shellac to dissolve.)

4- Shellac always has impurities that will have to be removed. Place a funnel with a piece of fine woven cloth or nylon stocking into a plastic bottle (with a squirt lid) and filter the liquid shellac. Close the bottle with the lid and make a note on the label with the date and concentration of the shellac.

5- Shellac is best applied with a finishing pad. To make one, place a tight ball of clean cotton strands or a rag in the center of a square piece of cotton cloth.

6- Grab the four corners of the cloth holding the ball and give them a twist so that they form a sort of handle.

7- The ball in the pad should be soaked with a generous amount of shellac. Then, the corners are twisted together and the excess liquid removed by pressing the pad on an absorbent paper towel.

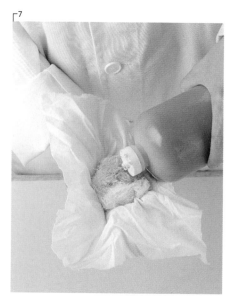

8-

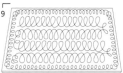

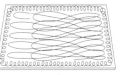

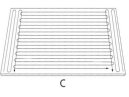

9- The shellac is applied with small figure-eight movements (A). As more coats are applied, the size of the figure-eight movements increases (B). The process is finished by making large zigzag movements (C), and the final coat is applied with long even strokes following the grain of the wood (D).

A

B

C

D

10- The finishing pad can be kept in perfect condition if it is put into a tightly sealed jar with a bit of alcohol after each use.

10

8- The shellac is applied by holding the twisted corners of the pad between the pinky and ring fingers and the palm of the hand. The thumb, index, and middle fingers act as a tripod, supporting the sides of the finishing pad.

Antique paint

The wood molding is prepared by brushing on a coat of acrylic sealer and leaving it to dry.

1- Next, a coat of a light-colored acrylic paint, in this case yellow, is applied with a narrow brush.

1

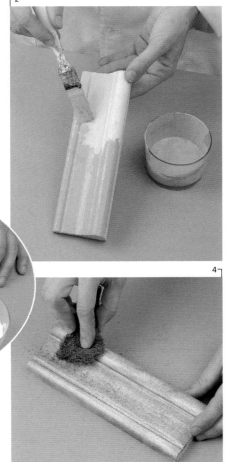

4

2- Before it has completely dried, a coat of bright-colored paint is added, a pastel pink in this case.

3- A commercial matte varnish is mixed with a small amount of burnt umber oil paint. The varnish is applied with a flat brush before the coat of paint has completely dried. The excess is removed by rubbing it with a cotton rag, then it is left to dry for half an hour.

4- The high areas of the molding are rubbed with a medium (number 00) steel wool pad. This will give it a worn look and will cause the different layers of color to show through the varnish, creating an aged effect.

Restoration

The restoration of furniture or any type of wood object requires a series of
well-defined processes: cleaning, disinfecting, reparation of parts, and
finishing. These processes vary greatly depending on the object being
treated and the type of wood and the problems it has. In this chapter,
a series of exercises illustrate the restoration of different pieces
of furniture with typical problems, similar to those that the
reader, without a doubt, will encounter. There are also
explanations of how to restore bamboo and wicker
objects, because these materials can develop
problems similar to those that affect wood.
In any case, the reader will be able to see
which processes are the most appropriate for his or her restoration project,
get ideas, and apply solutions
learned from one or several
exercises.

Decorating interiors with restored furniture

Throughout history, furniture has typically been expensive, but appreciated all the same. But it was during the nineteenth century that the appreciation of antique furniture and objects reached its highest point. The value (economic, aesthetic, sentimental, and so on) of a unique object made of high quality solid wood competes with the value (practical, design, economic, innovative, and so on) of mass produced industrial furniture made of new materials.

This restored desk decorates a hallway. Its undeniable aesthetic value is complemented by its practical value as a work table.

Where to find furniture for restoring

Furniture and objects in need of restoration can fall into our hands in many different ways. Those that are passed down to us from family members have great sentimental value, which can cause us to appreciate them even more than for their beauty or economic value. Friends or people we know may give us objects, which become part of our daily lives and always remind us of the person that gave them to us. It is also possible to buy objects and furniture that require restoration, or to save them from being discarded. In any case, before salvaging or acquiring any piece it is helpful to be able to discern an antique piece from an old one. Generally, an object is considered an antique when it is more than 100 years old, has a certain aesthetic quality, and is made from quality materials. Modernist and Art Deco pieces are also considered antiques. In the past few years, mass-produced objects made around 1950 have been included in this category, given their undeniable historic and aesthetic value. But the line that separates an antique from an old object is somewhat blurry and difficult to pin down, so we must let ourselves be guided by our taste and sensibility, by specialized manuals, or by the advice of professionals in the field before choosing a piece.

Furniture in need of restoration may also be acquired from dealers, who sell antique furniture and objects of lesser importance and recent periods, as well as old furniture pieces and objects with a certain degree of aesthetic appeal. There are also sellers at outdoor markets, public auctions, and flea markets where old furniture in various states of conservation may be purchased. Before acquiring or purchasing a piece to restore, it is important to make a general inspection to get an idea of its overall condition and the condition of the wood, and to estimate the amount of work that will be required for the restoration. The hidden parts and the back side should be examined, as well as the drawers, shelves, and moveable parts, which should be removed to verify their condition. The structure should be checked to make sure it is solid, the decorative parts examined, and the general condition of the wood and the finish inspected.

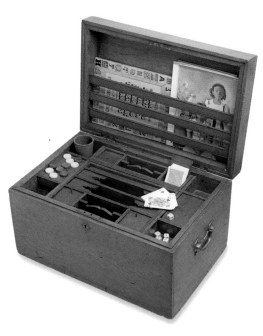

An antique trunk now is used for storing games and magazines.

The decor in this bedroom is based on the combination of antique furniture and modern accessories. The bed takes center stage, highlighted by modern pieces: aluminum shelves (designed by Oscar Tusquets) used as bedside tables and the small lamps.

Plate rack

Sometimes an object will be in "perfect" condition, provided that the normal wear and tear from use and the passage of time are taken into account. This plate rack is a good example. The wood is in perfect condition, aside from the layer of grime that has formed on its surface from daily use and the time spent in storage. Its restoration will focus on cleaning and bringing back the original patina of the different materials that make up the object: wood and sheet metal.

Rustic furniture, such as this plate rack, is usually constructed with thick boards, normally of pine or other softwoods, and they are not finished or covered at all. This is why it is possible to find such pieces in good condition. They have a solid structure, and usually the wood only requires cleaning and a final protective treatment.

A rustic plate rack constructed of pine and covered with sheet metal in certain areas. The piece is well made, and the wood is in good condition. There is a layer of grime, accumulated in the corners and grooves, and stains are also visible all over the surface. Under this layer is the natural patina of the wood. The sheet metal is an alloy of zinc and tin.

2- A scalpel or a sharp blade is used to remove traces of grime accumulated in the corners, gently scraping away from the body, keeping the other hand behind or on the knife if more pressure is needed. A cotton cloth can be used to wipe away the dirt. The area where the bars meet the frame should be thoroughly scrubbed with a brisk back and forth motion, using a piece of steel wool held with both hands.

3- It is a good idea not to use corrosive products to clean the metal parts. The zinc and tin alloy sheet has a natural coating that protects the metal and highlights its quality. Vegetable oil and tripoli are mixed in a container to make a thin, creamy paste. The oil will cover the metal with a fine film that will waterproof it but will not tarnish it. At the same time, the tripoli will remove the particles of dirt.
A swab is made by wrapping a piece of cotton ball around one end of a long stick.

4- The end of the swab is soaked in the cleaning solution. Then, it is dipped into the container of tripoli. The wet cotton will pick up a certain amount of the powder. The cleaning mixture alone is used to clean certain areas of the sheet metal that require a softer touch.

1- Surface dirt is eliminated without damaging the patina of the wood by dissolving the dirt with alcohol. A number 00 steel wool pad is soaked with 96 percent alcohol and used to thoroughly scrub the surface of the wood. It is important to scrub in the direction of the grain of the wood so it is not scratched or marked. Next, the surface is wiped with a clean cotton cloth to completely remove any traces of dirt. It is important to stop when the wood is clean but the patina is not removed. Excessive cleaning can leave the wood dull, without tone, quality, or authenticity.

5- The small areas of the metal are cleaned by scrubbing briskly with the swab. The cotton absorbs the dirt from the surface, so it is a good idea to change the cotton tips often. Next, all traces of the paste and tripoli powder are removed by wiping the clean area with a cotton ball soaked with vegetable oil.

6- The final treatment begins with the application of a thin coat of linseed oil using a clean cotton cloth. The first layer is left to dry until it is no longer tacky, at which time a second coat is applied. Linseed oil is a nontoxic, natural substance that is traditionally used for protecting rustic furniture.

7- Once the second coat is dry, the entire surface of the wood is buffed with very fine, 800-grit sandpaper. This will create a surface that is polished, even, smooth, and ready for the next application of oil.

8- Three more coats of linseed oil are applied, letting each one dry before the next application. Then the surface is polished by rubbing it with number 0000 steel wool.

9- It should be pointed out that linseed oil is flammable—that is to say, under certain environmental conditions it can self-combust if it is left out of its container. To avoid unpleasant incidents, any cotton with oil on it should be submerged in a container of water after the job has been finished.

10- The last step is to blend the finishes on the different surfaces by buffing them briskly with a clean cotton cloth. The pieces of wood that make up the plate rack are cut in different directions and therefore absorb the linseed oil differently. When buffed with the cloth, some areas become glossy while others are matte. Next, the sheet metal is wiped gently with a soft cloth to remove any remaining traces of oil.

11- This rustic style piece of furniture is now functional again thanks to restoration. The plate rack can be used for its original purpose, holding plates, or it can serve as a decorative piece for any corner, given the warmth of the patina of the wood.

Wood chest

Sometimes a piece of furniture that is in generally good condition can have certain problems with its surface. The most typical are dirt and grime and holes made by insects. The grime accumulated on the surface, along with the old wax, creates a matte coating that dulls the wood and makes the piece look bad. The insects that live in the wood leave very distinctive holes when they come out of it. They do not represent a problem in themselves, but they inspire a sense of decrepitude and lack of care, and ruin the beauty of the surface. This chest is a good example of both problems. Therefore the restoration will focus on eliminating the layer of dirty wax and any possible insects and filling all holes.

This rustic trunk is made of carved and stained pine. It has a solid structure, and the wood and the hardware are in good condition. There are holes on the outside caused by wood-boring insects, rust on the metal parts, and a layer of grime on the surface. There is a fair amount of dust and dirt in the interior.

1- Before beginning the restoration it must be determined whether the holes are recent and the insects are active. A commercial liquid disinfectant is applied to the inside of each hole with a syringe to eliminate them. This method will guarantee that the liquid will penetrate the openings and tunnels and reach the inside of the wood, where the insects are living. Latex gloves and a respirator rated for organic fumes must be worn for protection.

2- Next the trunk is placed in the center of a sheet of polyethylene plastic, large enough for the piece of furniture. A disinfecting bag is made by closing the sides of the plastic with packing tape, making sure not to leave any openings. Several moth pellets are placed inside, and the bag is sealed. Finally, the date is written on a piece of paper or cardboard and attached to one of the sides of the bag, which is then left for 15 days.

3- The bag is removed after the time required for disinfection. The preliminary cleaning is done by removing the dust accumulated in the corners and interior surfaces, and on the underside and rear of the trunk with a household vacuum cleaner on its highest setting. The trunk is turned over and the underside is cleaned thoroughly, because it is very dirty from having contact with the floor.

4- The cleaning of the interior is finished with a thorough buffing of the wood's surface using a cotton cloth soaked with 96 percent alcohol until the layer of grime is completely removed.

⌐1

⌐3

⌐2
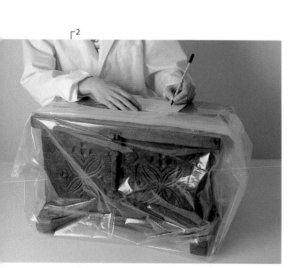

⌐4

⌐5

5- The exterior of the trunk also needs a deep cleaning with some type of abrasive product to eliminate the grime. A liquid cleaner is made by mixing 8 ounces (250 ml) of turpentine with 1 teaspoon of powdered rottenstone in a glass container and shaking it until a whitish liquid is formed. The wood is cleaned by scrubbing small areas of the surface in a circular pattern with a piece of cotton soaked with the cleaning solution. Special attention is paid to the carved surfaces, because it is important to clean all the areas well.

6- The oxidation is removed from the hardware (keyhole and braces) by scrubbing them with number 00 steel wool. This helps restore the deep black color and quality of the forged iron.

7- Melted wax is used to fill the holes. First, a bar of solid wax the same color as the wood is chosen. Then a small torch set on low is held with one hand, and a few drops of wax are melted from the bar, which is held with the other hand over the area. The liquid drops fall and run into the hole. The end of the torch is used to flatten the wax, until it is level with the surface of the wood. If the drops of wax do not fall into the holes or are not level with the surface of the wood, they can be removed by lightly rubbing them with fine sandpaper.

8- When all holes have been filled, the piece of furniture is ready to be waxed. A coat of colorless furniture wax is applied to the entire surface of the wood chest, as well as to the iron pieces. Then it is left to dry completely.

9- The surface of the wood is buffed with a cotton cloth or the wool finishing pad from an electric drill (as in this case) in the direction of the grain to create an even, deep, satiny gloss. Special attention should be given to the metal pieces, the feet, and molding, which tend to be less shiny because of their material and location.

10- The result is a piece of furniture that is free from surface imperfections and that has recovered its original beauty.

Side table

It is common for a restorer to encounter a piece of furniture whose various components or entire sections are made from more than one kind of wood. Because their innate characteristics differ, each wood reacts differently to the finish treatment. This is why, in most cases, the surface is treated beforehand to unify them. The table whose restoration is illustrated in the following exercise is a good example of such a case because it is made of solid beech with an oak veneer. Another common problem is that many pieces of furniture have ugly stains on their legs or on the parts that have had contact with the floor. They are difficult to remove, and special tools are required. Besides concealing imperfections and removing the marks left by insects, the restoration of this side table will focus on unifying the different wood surfaces, removing stains from the legs, and providing a quality finish.

This side table is made of beech and oak veneer. The legs and the frame are made of solid beech whereas the tabletop (also beech) is veneered with oak. The coat of varnish is in bad condition: It has turned completely matte, it is dark in some areas, and it has disappeared from others. The surface has holes from wood-boring insects.

1- The restoration begins by disassembling the table. The screws that hold the tabletop to the frame are not original to the piece and are quite rusted, so they are removed with a screwdriver. Because the screws are in poor condition, they will not be reused when the piece is restored, so they are discarded.

2- A commercial stripping product in gel form is used to remove the old varnish from the wood. A coat is applied to the entire surface of the table with a brush. Neoprene gloves, cotton clothing, eye protection, and a respirator must be used as a precaution. Good ventilation is also recommended if the work is done indoors.

3- The stripper is left on for several minutes until the varnish softens and forms a paste. Next, it is removed from the surface of the tabletop with a paint scraper, pressing lightly while moving it in the direction of the grain of the wood. The paste is wiped off onto a piece of newspaper. Then, the wood is wiped with a cotton cloth soaked with solvent. On small or curved surfaces a number 00 steel wool pad soaked with solvent is used to remove the stripping agent completely.

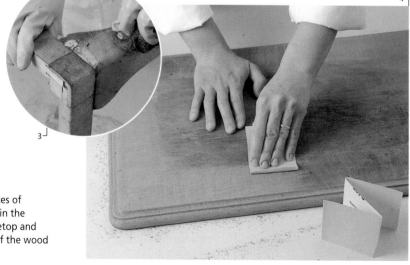

4- A thorough sanding of the table will eliminate any traces of varnish still adhered to the surface and any imperfections in the wood before the finish is applied. First, the veneered tabletop and the areas are lightly rubbed in the direction of the grain of the wood with a piece of 220-grit sandpaper.

5- Then, the curved areas are sanded, rubbing the wood in the direction of the grain with a sanding sponge. The sponge is flexible, so it will adapt to the shape of the wood.

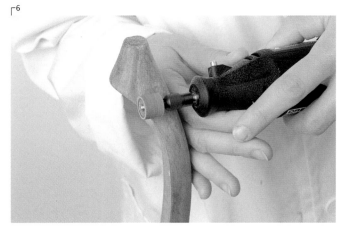

6- The lower parts of the legs have the characteristic stains caused by continuous use and contact with the floor. Hand sanding is not enough to remove them, so a rotary tool is used. The darkened areas are sanded using the rotary tool, with an aluminum oxide tip, until a color similar to that of the rest of the leg appears. The job is completed by wiping the wood with a cotton cloth to remove the sawdust.

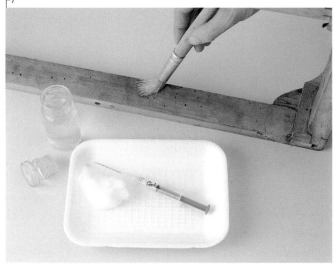

7- The wood is disinfected after the varnish has been completely removed and the entire piece is sanded. First, the liquid is injected into every hole with a syringe. Then, a coat of disinfectant is applied to all surfaces with a brush. A respirator and gloves are recommended if there is a chance that the liquid will come into contact with the skin.

8- Finally, the table is wrapped in flexible plastic. This procedure has an effect similar to that of the disinfecting bag because it creates a disinfectant-saturated atmosphere. A piece of paper with the date is attached to the plastic and left for 15 days, which is just long enough to kill the insects.

9- After 15 days, the finishing process begins. Because the table is made of two different kinds of woods, oak and beech, a special process is used on the oak veneer to blend the surfaces. A coat of filler is applied with a wide brush, following the predominant direction of the wood grain. It is necessary to use latex gloves and a respirator because the filler is quite toxic.

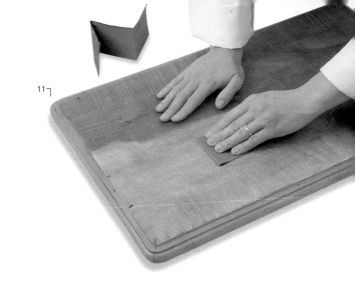

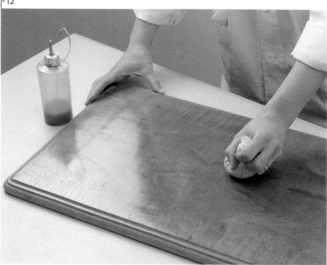

10- The filler coat is quickly wiped with a cotton cloth folded to form a pad to eliminate any brush marks or accumulated filler. Then the surface is left to dry.

11- The process is finished by sanding the wood in the direction of the grain until the surface is soft and smooth to the touch. Then it is briskly buffed with 360-grit sandpaper and wiped with a cotton cloth to remove the dust.

12- Shellac is chosen for the final treatment because of its glossy finish. The furniture piece is placed in a dust-free area. A pad is charged with shellac, and the surface of the wood is lightly rubbed with small figure-eight motions. Gradually, the motions are increased in size until they end up as zigzags and then straight wiping motions in the direction of the grain of the wood. Several coats are applied, and then the shellac is left to dry completely.

13- A wax similar in color to the wood is mixed to conceal the holes that the insects made. Pure beeswax (enough to fill all holes) is mixed in a metal container with a half teaspoon of powdered pigment, in this case raw sienna. The mixture is warmed on a hot plate, stirring to make a fluid paste with a uniform color.

14- The warm wax is applied to every hole by taking a small amount from the container on the hot plate with the tip of a spatula or spoon and dripping it into the hole.

15- Before the wax hardens, the surface is smoothed with a wooden spatula. The end of a wooden clothespin can be used instead of the spatula, as is done here.

16- Once this process is completed, the table is assembled. The legs are attached to the frame with new screws, because the originals were rusty and had stained the wood.

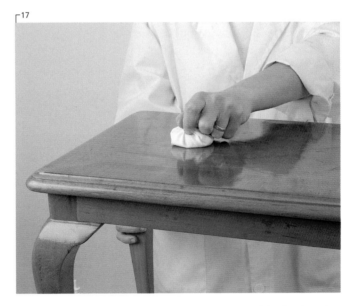

17- Finally, the last coats of shellac are applied to blend the finishes of the different surfaces—and the more coats of shellac applied, the deeper and glossier the finish.

18- The original color of the woods has been restored. The table stands out because of its high-quality finish.

Bamboo chair

Sometimes furniture pieces undergo changes after they come out of the factory. It is not unusual to find furniture that has been varnished or painted with dark colors after it has been used for a while or when new, depending on personal taste or the fad of the moment. These pieces are generally in good condition, because the coat of paint or varnish has protected the surface. A good example is this chair made of bamboo and wicker. Both of these fibers are commonly used to make light outdoor furniture, and both materials can be treated as if they were wood—in fact, they can be restored in the same way.

The restoration of this chair focuses on the removal of the paint with a stripper and the protection of the bamboo with two coats of finish, to restore the original look of the piece.

This bamboo chair is in good condition because it has been covered with several coats of black enamel paint. Bamboo is not a very porous material; it does not accept paint well unless the bamboo has been prepared beforehand. In this case, the paint was applied directly over the bamboo, and because of that it has begun to peel and come off in the areas of heavy use.

1- A gel stripping agent is used to remove the thick coats of enamel. The chair is placed outdoors on sawhorses, and the gel is applied beginning with one area, in this case the legs, the stretchers, and the underside of the seat. Neoprene gloves, heavy cotton clothing, and a respirator should be worn for protection.

2- Following the manufacturer's instructions on the container, the stripper is left to work for several minutes, until the coat of paint softens and acquires a pasty consistency that forms a wrinkled and uneven surface. Then, the paint is washed off with a stream of water from the garden hose.

3- The rest of the paint that clings to the bamboo knots or to the backs of the legs is removed by scrubbing with a kitchen pad and rinsing the area with plenty of water.

4- A single coat of stripper is not sufficient to remove the paint from the inside corners of the chair. A second coat is applied, paying special attention to the joints made of strips of wicker and the grooves in the cane. Then the paint is removed by scrubbing in different directions with a vegetable fiber brush and flushing the area with water. After finishing this process, the other half of the chair (the back and the top of the seat) is stripped following the same procedure.

5- Once the entire chair has been stripped, the work can be continued indoors. While the chair is still damp, but not dripping water, a generous amount of 96 percent alcohol is applied to all surfaces with a clean cotton cloth. This step will ensure the removal of any traces of stripping gel, and at the same time it will help the water on the surface to evaporate.

6- Alcohol-based varnish is mixed with a commercial stain, also alcohol based, in a wide-mouthed glass jar. The amounts will vary according to the desired tone, but it is a good idea to be cautious with the stain and to test the mixture several times before using it. The varnish with the stain is applied with a brush to darken the whitish tone of the stripped bamboo and then is left to dry. If the chair is to be used outdoors, an exterior-grade varnish, tinted as explained above, should be used.

7- Once the varnish has dried, a protective coat of furniture wax is applied with a cotton cloth. The wax is left to dry completely, according to the manufacturer's instructions indicated on the container.

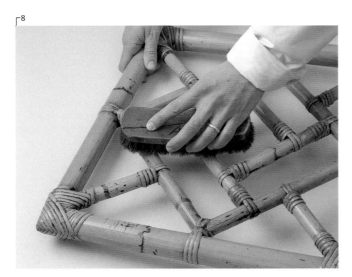

8- The surface of the bamboo is polished by buffing it thoroughly with a soft clothes brush. The result will be a characteristic deep, satiny shine.

9- The finished chair has recovered its attractive original look, much in line with the latest trends in interior decoration, which promote a return to natural materials.

Sewing stand, made of solid oak and oak veneer on the tops of the lids. It has a thick coat of grime as a result of a poor waxing job done over an old layer of varnish. Also, parts have come unglued, and hardware is in poor condition.

Sewing stand

Furniture that requires restoration frequently has structural problems resulting from the wear and tear caused by daily use. Pieces that have come unglued, hardware that has rusted, and parts that have loose joints are some of the most typical problems. If these problems all occur at the same time, the furniture piece will be fragile, the structure will come apart, and the piece will not survive daily use.

This sewing stand is a good example of this problem. The restoration will have to focus on disassembling the object completely and carefully assembling it by gluing, fitting, nailing, or screwing the pieces as they were originally.

In this case, the structure has been reinforced by gluing the loose parts and replacing the fasteners that were in poor condition. The coat of grime that covered the surface, which was the result of an unfortunate intervention after the piece was manufactured, has also been removed.

1- The first step of the restoration is to disassemble the piece. The screws that hold the movable parts to the base of the stand are removed. They are unscrewed and carefully separated, numbering the pieces with adhesive labels according to their placement in the stand. The insides of the trays are also marked with the same number as their corresponding wood connectors. A sketch can be drawn on a piece of paper or the numbering order can be noted.

⌐1

⌐2

⌐3

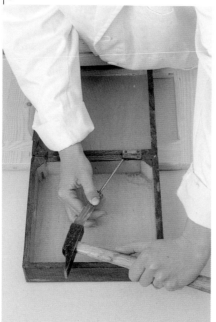

2- The legs that have come unglued are removed. A thick piece of wood is held with one hand against the joint of the leg and the frame of the stand, located at the inside corner. Then, the wood is struck hard with a nylon-headed mallet, which is held in the other hand. This will break the joint and knock the leg free. The wood block will protect the stand from possible dents and scratches caused by the mallet.

3- The disassembly process continues as the hinges of the two top trays are removed. The open tray is positioned near the body, and it is held this way, placing a piece of wood between the person and the tray. The hinges are attached with small brads; to remove them a screwdriver with a small, narrow tip is placed between the hinge and the wood. The handle of the screwdriver is tapped with a hammer while prying with a lever motion.

4- The brads are pulled out with pincers. Special care is taken not to cut the heads off, because that would make it difficult to remove them.

5- A gel stripping agent is used to remove the thick coating of grime that covers the entire surface of the stand. The piece is placed in a well-ventilated area, and neoprene gloves and a respirator are used for protection. A thick coat of stripper is applied to the surface of the stand with a wide brush, and it is put aside until the coat of grime has softened.

6- The layer of paste formed by the stripper mixed with the varnish and the wax is removed by scraping it in the direction of the grain of the wood while applying light pressure. The paste is wiped on a piece of newspaper.

7- The rest of the stripper is removed by scrubbing the wood in the direction of the grain with a number 00 steel wool pad soaked with solvent.

8- The wood is scrubbed with a cotton cloth soaked with 96 percent alcohol until the surface is free from all traces of solvent and stripper.

9- Once all exterior surfaces have been stripped, the interiors are cleaned. The wood is briskly scrubbed with a number 00 steel wool pad soaked with 96 percent alcohol until the grime is removed. Then, the surface is wiped with a cotton cloth.

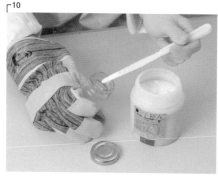

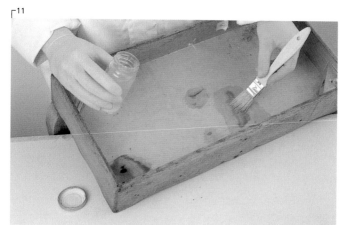

11- The warm solution is applied generously over the ink stains with a brush and left to dry. The water evaporates and the oxalic acid remains crystallized on the surface, forming a powdery coating.

10- The inside of the base of the stand has ink stains that were not removed during the preliminary cleaning. A solution of oxalic acid and water is used to remove them. The solution is prepared by mixing some hot water (enough to be able to apply a generous amount to the stains) in a glass jar, with small amounts of oxalic acid while stirring. The solution will be ready when it becomes supersaturated—that is, when the oxalic acid precipitates to the bottom of the jar. The use of a respirator, latex gloves, and heavy work gloves are required when handling the jar with the hot water.

12- The oxalic acid crystals are removed by scrubbing the surface with a clean cotton cloth soaked with plenty of water, and then left to dry. Because the action of the water on the surface raises the grain of the wood, it must be rubbed with 220-grit sandpaper.

13- Before any part or piece of furniture is glued, it is important to make sure that there are no traces of old adhesive, because this can weaken the newly glued joints. The leg is held on a work table with a clamp, inserting small pieces of wood or rubber (as in this case) between the metal and the wood to avoid possible scratches or marks. The layer of old glue is removed by scraping it with a chisel.

14- Another method for removing the layers of old glue is to soften the adhesive with solvent or water or both. Then, it is removed by scraping with a scalpel or sharp knife. The leg is held with one hand while the tool is guided with the other.

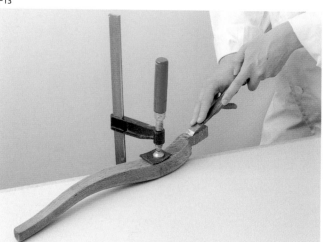

15- White carpenter's glue is used to attach the legs. A coat is applied with a brush to the top of the piece that is to be inserted into the base of the stand.

16- The leg and the block are inserted into the base and held with a clamp. A piece of rubber is placed between the clamp and the surface of the furniture to avoid possible scratches and marks. The glued pieces are left to dry for 12 hours.

17- After the 12 hours have passed, the stand is ready for finishing. First, the surface is prepared by applying a coat of shellac with a wide brush.

18- Next, powdered wax is sprinkled over the surface of the wood. Using a polishing pad saturated with colorless furniture wax, the wax is spread and rubbed into the wood with large circular movements.

19- The final assembly of the stand begins by consulting the sketch or the instructions written at the beginning of the restoration process. The numbered stickers are used as references for the correct placement of the side crosspieces. The trays from one side of the table are assembled first.

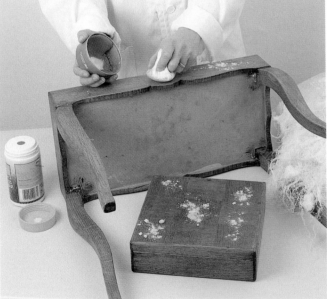

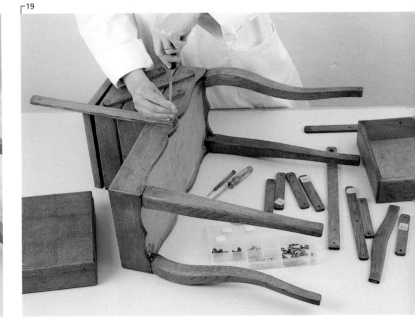

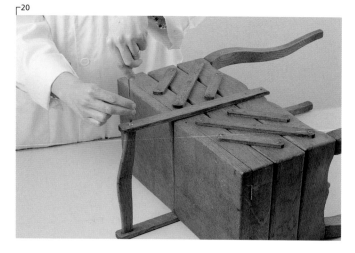

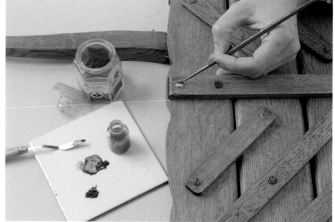

20- The trays of the other side are assembled, and then the central handle attached. The screws and washers that were oxidized and that could stain the wood have been replaced by similar new ones. The hinges of the lids have been changed for the same reason.

21- The new screws and washers are shiny and contrast with the original ones, which produces an unpleasant effect. A mixture of shellac and a natural dark-colored pigment is applied to the pieces with a number 2 sable hair retouching brush to make them blend.

22- The last step includes cleaning and attaching the pulls. To clean them they are placed tightly in the jaws of a bench vise, held snugly between small pieces of wood or clothespins (as in this case). Then, they are cleaned using a small rotary tool with a metal polishing attachment. Finally, they are screwed to the sides of the top trays.

23- The restoration concludes with the buffing of all the different surfaces of the stand with a cotton cloth until they shine.

24- The resulting piece is a sewing stand with a strong structure that will withstand daily use. The original color, shine, and quality of the oak have been restored.

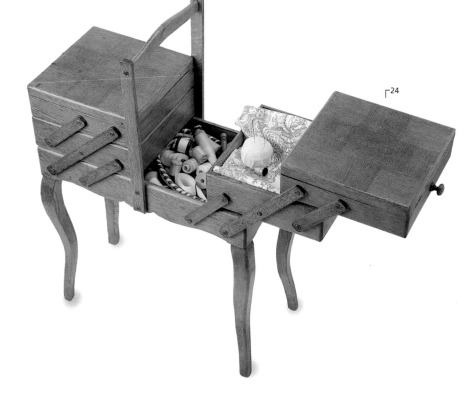

Wicker umbrella stand

Furniture and objects made of cane and wicker usually have the same problems as those made of wood, because the damaging factors are similar. The worst of these are mildew and insects. Mildew is a common problem in pieces made of wicker. This material swells when it comes in contact with water or excessive humidity, causing parts of the object to break or come apart and encouraging mildew. In the case at hand, the surface of the umbrella stand has a coating of mold, caused by mildew, and the base has come apart due to water damage.

The restoration will take place in phases: the first will consist of disinfecting the wicker and completely removing the layer of mold using a dry-cleaning technique. Next, the base will be attached, and finally, a finish will be applied to protect the surface of the object.

Wicker umbrella stand, which is in mediocre condition. The base has separated from the stand because the glue has come off. The wicker strips that form the stand are in good condition. Although no breaks or fragmentation is apparent, mold covers the entire surface.

The entire surface of the umbrella stand has been attacked by mold—that is, the greenish color and dusty texture that covers the wicker. The infestation is worse in the corners and angles, especially where the strips cross each other and at the places where different pieces join, for example, where the rings meet the body.

1- The first step consists of eliminating the mold. The body and base of the umbrella stand are placed on a sheet of polyethylene plastic. Next, a glass container, for example a drinking glass, is placed inside the stand with a small amount of solid thymol. Then, the plastic is cut, the object is wrapped, and the sides are closed with packing tape, making sure that there are no openings to spoil the hermetically sealed disinfecting bag. Finally, the date is written on a piece of paper or cardboard and attached to one of the sides of the bag. The piece is left for 15 days.

2- After 15 days (necessary to ensure that the mold completely disappears), the disinfecting bag is removed. Then, the surface of the wicker is cleaned, removing the dust, the dirt, and any traces of mold with a household vacuum cleaner at its highest setting, using the brush attachment. A soft bristle brush is used to scrub the corners and joints of the woven wicker to loosen the layer of dust and mold.

3- The next step is dry cleaning with soap to eliminate all traces of mold and grime. Using a large glass container with a lid, 75% distilled water and 25% neutral liquid soap (pH 7) is mixed, in a quantity not to exceed one-fourth of the total volume of the container. The container is closed and briskly shaken, mixing it until a thick foam appears on top. A small amount of the foam is taken from the container with a toothbrush, which is used to scrub the wicker until the layer of grime has been eliminated.

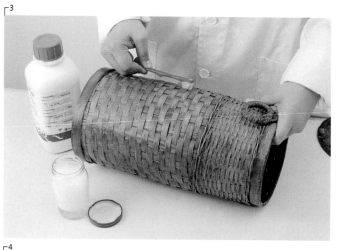

4- The surface of the umbrella stand is then rinsed to remove any soap residue. A towel or terry cloth mitten is lightly dampened with distilled water, and the wicker is scrubbed in all directions, paying special attention to the joints and the corners of the woven material.

5- As it has been pointed out, the wicker tends to swell when wet. It must be dried immediately. The most practical solution is to use a hairdryer set on the coldest setting.

6- The base of the umbrella stand was attached to the body with a commercial, all-purpose glue. It is a good idea to eliminate any traces of it before a new adhesive is applied. The glue is softened with acetone applied with a cotton ball wrapped around the ends of a pair of large tweezers. The fragments of old glue are lifted and removed with a scalpel (as in this case), a sharp knife or a razor blade.

7- The base is attached using a transparent, all-purpose glue following the instructions on the package. This kind of adhesive is reversible and easily removed with acetone, making it very appropriate for this type of restoration.

8- The base is fitted to the body of the umbrella stand and pressure is applied to hold it in place. A weight or any heavy object can be used to apply pressure to the base. It is a good idea to place a piece of paper (as in this case), rubber, or wood between the object and the weight to prevent scratches or marks. The adhesive is left to dry for 24 hours.

9- After 24 hours, a finish is applied that will both beautify and protect the wicker. A coat of liquid furniture wax is applied with a wide soft brush and left to dry.

10- The entire surface is buffed with a clothes brush until it has acquired an even satin sheen.

11- The final result is an attractive umbrella stand, well conserved and strong, returned to the practical use for which it was created, while also providing decoration for the entry of the house.

Wall rack

Frequently, veneered objects and furniture pieces will have broken and lost pieces of veneer. The thin pieces of wood (the veneer) are extremely sensitive to changes in temperature and humidity that can cause expansion or contraction that result in breakage. A broken piece ends up coming off the backing, and if not noticed on time, it is lost forever. Veneer is very sensitive to rough use, especially those pieces located at the edges and corners of the furniture piece. Repairing missing areas by replacing them with new veneer is a typical task in the restoration of these types of objects.

The wall rack that will be restored here has an area whose veneer is missing. It will be repaired following the classic method. A quick process for replacing veneer with straight sides will be demonstrated as well. Following that, the color of the new veneer will be blended to match the original wood. Finally, the wood will be protected and embellished with a high-quality finish matching the style of the object.

The pine wall rack is covered with walnut veneer and boxwood marquetry. The piece has an old layer of varnish that is in poor condition. This clouds the surface, causing the color of the wood to be different from the original, with no sheen. A small piece of veneer is missing at the edge near one of the knobs. Also noticeable are the many holes made by insects.

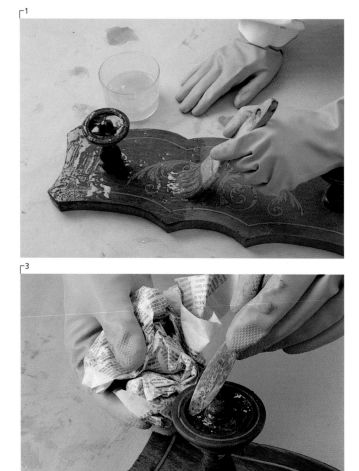

1- The first step, which must be carried out before any other task, consists of stripping the rack completely. The protection of long neoprene gloves and a respirator are required for handling the stripping agent. The gel is applied to the entire surface of the object with a brush and left until the varnish softens.

2- The paste formed by the action of the stripper on the varnish is removed from the flat surfaces with a scraper. It is then wiped on a piece of newspaper held in the other hand.

3- A metal spatula with a rounded end is used to remove the paste from the curved areas. This tool can clean all hard-to-reach areas without scratching the wood. As before, the paste can be wiped onto newspaper. Once all of the surfaces have been completely cleaned, a number 00 steel wool pad soaked with solvent is used to remove any traces of the stripper from the wood.

4- The rack is left to dry completely. Then the wood is immediately sanded, rubbing in the direction of the grain with a number 00 steel wool pad to remove traces of stripper and to smooth the surface. A flexible sponge that adapts to the shape of the object is used to sand curved areas. Finally, the resulting dust is wiped away with a cotton cloth.

5- It can be observed that the insects are no longer active. To prevent new infestations, a commercial disinfectant is injected into all of the holes using a syringe to make sure it penetrates the wood. A coat of disinfectant is also applied to the surface of the rack with a brush. Protective gloves and a respirator should be worn in case the disinfectant comes into direct contact with the hands.

6- Then, the missing piece of veneer is repaired. First the wood near the missing area is cut to make the edges straight. The cut is made leaving the maximum amount of veneer intact, cutting away the least possible surface. A straight-edge is placed on the surface of the hanger, and using it as a guide, a small fragment of veneer is cut with a scalpel or a sharp knife.

7- Another method of straightening the edge of the broken area consists of making a cut with a blade. The sharp edge of the tool is placed on the surface of the wood and the back of it is given a sharp tap with a hammer. The piece of veneer will come away, and the cut will be perfectly straight.

8- Next, the area that is to be repaired is traced, and this will be used as a pattern for cutting the new veneer. A piece of carbon paper is taped to the surface of the wood with the clean side down, and a thin piece of paper is placed over it. A perfect tracing of the required piece is made by rubbing the area with the handle of any tool. Then, a piece of veneer as similar as possible to the wood of the wall rack is selected.

9- The white paper with the tracing is placed right-side up on the selected piece of veneer, and paying special attention to the direction of the grain of the wood it is adhered with hot rabbit skin glue. Then several pieces of paper are glued to the underside of the veneer, to stiffen and strengthen it.

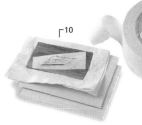

10- Two pieces of any type of veneer are cut to the size of the papers and placed under them as a backing. Masking tape is used to hold the edges of the different pieces together, making a small packet that will be comfortable to work with.

11- The next step consists of cutting the veneer following the outline of the pattern. The veneer packet is placed on a wood base, and using a pocket-size hand drill with a very small bit, a hole is made at one of the corners of the tracing.

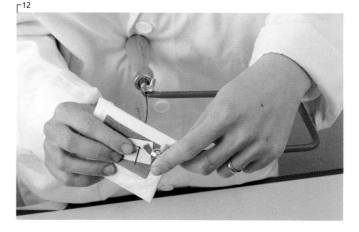

12- A fine marquetry blade is attached to one side of a piercing saw. The end of the blade is passed through the previously drilled hole and then attached to the other end of the saw.

13- The veneer packet is held on a workbench or on two slightly separated boards and cut, very carefully, following the outline of the shape. Only the piece of veneer required for the repair is saved.

14- The process is completed by gluing the veneer to the base. Hot rabbit skin glue is applied with a medium-sized brush to the back of the piece with the tracing attached and to the wall rack as well.

15- The veneer is placed over the area being repaired and covered with a couple of pieces of clean paper. Thin pieces of wood are inserted between the rack and the clamp, and the clamp is then tightened to apply pressure to the veneer that is being glued. The pieces of wood protect the rack from marks and scratches, and the paper will keep the new veneer from adhering to the wood pieces if any of the glue seeps out. The rack is left to dry for 24 hours.

16- After 24 hours, the clamp is released and the paper covering the new veneer is removed. The surface is rubbed with a cotton cloth slightly dampened with tap water, to help take the paper off. Then the area is left to dry completely.

17- It is possible to use another technique that is quicker but equally effective for repairing missing veneer. After the tracing has been made as described before, it is glued to the front (the side that will be visible when the process is finished) of the selected piece with a thin coat of transparent, all-purpose glue.

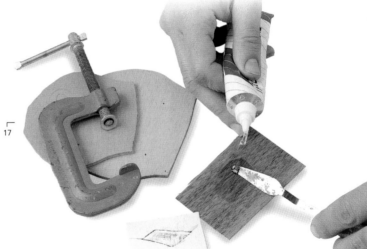

18- The shape is carefully cut out with a pair of sharp scissors. Then, the back of the veneer (the side without paper) is attached to the base with all-purpose glue and is held in place with a clamp following the procedure described before. The adhesive is left to dry for 12 hours. Finally, the paper covering the new veneer is removed, rubbing its surface with a cotton cloth dampened with acetone to help the paper come off. This procedure is practical when the veneer has straight edges and clean angles that are easy to cut with scissors.

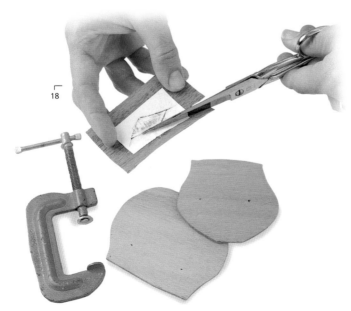

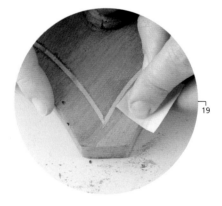

19- The new piece of veneer is thoroughly sanded by rubbing it briskly with 180-grit sandpaper until the surface is smooth and polished and ready for finishing.

20- Before the finish is applied to the rack, a test is made to determine the color the new veneer will be after it has been varnished. The area in question is rubbed with cotton balls dampened with alcohol. There is an obvious difference in the tones, making it necessary to stain the new piece.

21- A coat of commercial solvent-based stain that has been heavily diluted is applied to the solid wood knobs to match the tone of the veneer. A flat brush is used for this application, and then any streaks are removed by wiping with a cotton rag. The wood is left to dry.

22- The same commercial solvent-based stain, undiluted, is applied to the new veneer with a fine, soft retouching brush and left to dry.

23- Finishing begins with an application of shellac, which acts as a base for the wax. In a dust-free space, the shellac is applied with a finishing pad in successive layers, allowing them to dry after each application. The first layers are applied with small figure-eight motions. Then the movements become gradually larger, changing to zigzag motions and ending with horizontal strokes.

24- Special attention is paid to curved areas of the knob, which tend to shine less because of their shape.

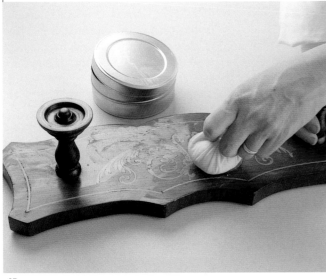

25- Next, a coat of homemade wax is applied to the entire surface of the rack. It is rubbed with circular motions to make sure that it penetrates deeply into the wood. It is left to dry and then buffed with a clean cotton cloth until the piece is evenly shiny.

26- The insect holes are filled before the last coat is applied. Two bars of shellac similar in color to the wood of the veneer and of the marquetry are selected. An electric burn-in knife set on warm will be used. While the bar of shellac is held over a hole with one hand, the burn-in knife is held near it with the other; drops of liquid shellac fall and cover the holes. The shellac is allowed to solidify, and the excess is removed with the tip of a scalpel.

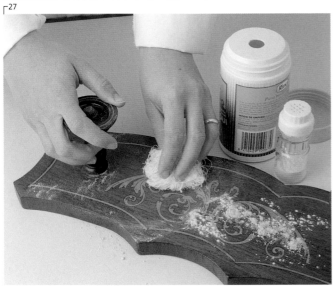

27- The process is concluded by sprinkling rottenstone and powdered wax on the surface of the rack, and then briskly rubbing it with a clean cotton cloth. The rottenstone and wax combine to give the wood a deep gloss.

28- The restored wall rack has been returned to its original condition. The soft satin finish of the wood adds warmth to the entryway where it hangs.

This chair is made of stained beech. The wood is in good condition: The only problems are a coat of old varnish and a few holes caused by wood-boring insects. The upholstered seat is the part that is in the worst condition: The fabric is dirty and discolored, and it has holes in it; the decorative gimp is frayed, and the structure is not very firm.

1- The first step consists of completely taking the seat apart. The decorative gimp is removed, and the tacks holding the fabric are pulled out by inserting the blade of a chisel between them and the wood and striking them with a hammer until they come loose. Then the fabric is removed and discarded.

2- The same steps are followed to remove the sackcloth that covers the springs. The tacks are removed with a nail puller: The points on the end of the tool are forced under the head of the tack, and a lever motion causes the tacks to come loose. Finally, the sackcloth is removed and discarded.

Upholstered chair

Sometimes, furniture pieces with upholstery need to be restored. Upholstery is a complex trade that requires apprenticeship, skill, and practice. However, it is possible for any person to restore furniture that has upholstered parts. Such restoration almost always requires the replacement of fabric (which usually has holes and tears), rusted elements (springs and tacks), and broken elements (sackcloth). In any case, an intervention should always respect the original upholstery techniques: a spring system should never be replaced with foam rubber padding, for example.

This chair has a heavy coating of old varnish that is in poor condition, and the structure of the upholstery has completely come apart. The restoration will consist of removing the varnish, replacing the upholstery, and applying a finish to the wood.

3- The nail puller is also used to remove the webbing from under the seat. In this case, the tacks have been inserted so deeply into the wood that a hammer must be used to strike the handle of the tool to drive the tip between the wood and the tack. Then the twine that attaches the bottoms of the springs to the webbing is cut.

4- The twine that holds the springs is taken apart, and the tacks that hold it to the frame are removed with pincers. The old webbing and springs are discarded.

5- Next, work begins on the wood, which is completely stripped to remove the layer of old varnish. A coat of gel stripper is applied to the entire chair with a flat brush. Long neoprene gloves, heavy cotton clothing, and a respirator are worn for protection. It is a good idea to do this outdoors or in a well-ventilated place.

6- Some time is allowed to let the varnish soften. A paint scraper is used to remove the paste (made of stripper and varnish) from the chair. The paste is scraped off with one hand and wiped onto a piece of old newspaper held in the other hand.

7- A nooker knife is used to remove the paste from the grooves in the carvings and molding. This tool will efficiently remove all the traces of paste from the grooves.

8- Any remnants of the stripper are removed by scrubbing the surface of the wood with a number 00 steel wool pad soaked with solvent. Then it is left to dry.

9- A suede brush with soft metal bristles is used to clean traces of the paste from the grooves in the carving. The wood is briskly brushed to remove all of the stripper.

10- Then the surface of the chair is thoroughly sanded with 180-grit sandpaper, to prepare it for the final treatment. Special attention is paid to the areas with carvings and molding, folding the paper to insert it in the grooves and sanding thoroughly.

11- The sandpaper will not work in some of the carved decorations, so it will be necessary to use a nooker knife.

12- The holes caused by insects do not have any of the characteristic sawdust, which indicates that they are no longer active. However, as a preventive measure, a disinfecting liquid is applied to the holes, using a syringe to ensure that it penetrates deeply into the wood. Protective gloves and a respirator should be used if there is a chance that the disinfectant will come into contact with the hands.

14- A coat of shellac is applied and left to dry. This layer will act as a base for the final coat of shellac.

13- The stripping and subsequent sanding of the chair have eliminated the coat of walnut-colored varnish, so it will be necessary to stain it again to return it to its original condition. A commercial solvent-based stain of the same color will be used. It can be applied with a flat brush, completely covering all of the wood, and then wiped clean with a cotton cloth to blend the layer of color and to remove any brush marks. The wood is left to dry completely.

15- Next, shellac is applied with a finishing pad. In a dust-free environment, the shellac is put on in successive layers, which are allowed to dry between applications. The first ones are rubbed with small figure-eight motions, slowly getting larger until they turn into horizontal strokes.

16- After the finish has been applied, all of the insect holes are covered. A bar of wax of a color similar to that of the wood is selected and a small amount kneaded with the fingers, making a cylindrical shape.

17- Part of the wax is inserted into the hole.

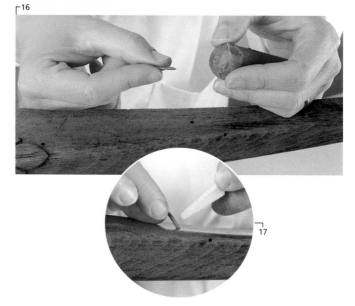

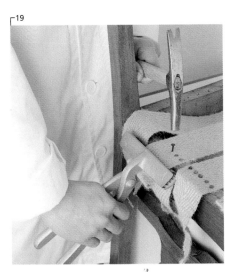

18- The piece of wax is flattened with a wood spatula or the tip of a clothespin (as in this case), covering the hole and wiping it from the surface of the chair.

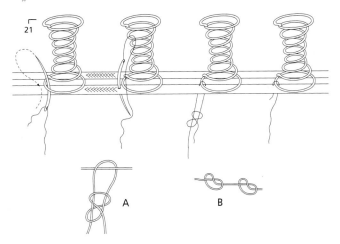

19- After the wood has been restored, attention is directed to the upholstery, which will be constructed with all new materials, faithfully following the original work. First, the base is created attaching four webbing strips with tacks to the underside of the frame of the chair's seat. Next, they are pulled tight using pliers for stretching canvas, and they are tacked to the opposite side of the frame. The operation is repeated, weaving four webbing strips perpendicular to the other four, tacking them at the two opposite sides of the underside of the seat.

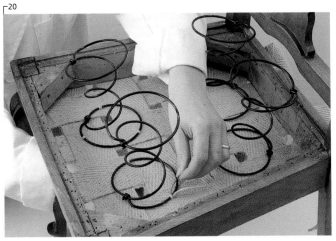

20- Four springs are centered on the base and sewn to the webbing with an upholstery needle and twine.

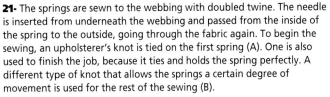

21- The springs are sewn to the webbing with doubled twine. The needle is inserted from underneath the webbing and passed from the inside of the spring to the outside, going through the fabric again. To begin the sewing, an upholsterer's knot is tied on the first spring (A). One is also used to finish the job, because it ties and holds the spring perfectly. A different type of knot that allows the springs a certain degree of movement is used for the rest of the sewing (B).

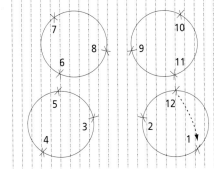

22- Each spring is sewn at three points, following the order indicated by the numbers. This system is effective for holding the springs.

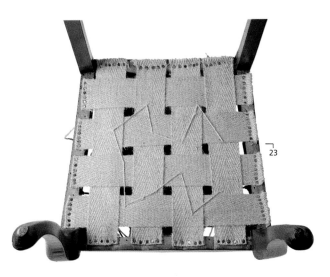

23- View of the underside of the chair with the webbing and sewing patterns.

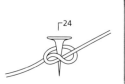

24- The upper part of the springs are tied with cord to hold and stabilize them. First a tack is set in one side of the chair's frame, aligned with the center of one of the springs. Then, one end of the cord is tied around the spring and, finally, the tack is driven all the way in.

25- The first knot of each spring is lined up with the head of a tack, using this kind of fixed knot.

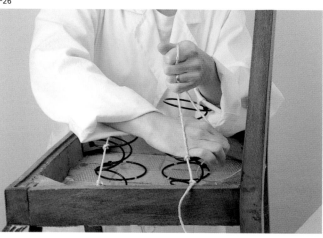

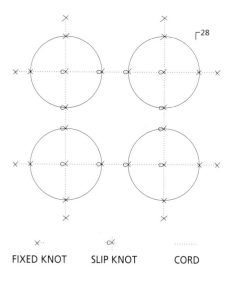

FIXED KNOT	SLIP KNOT	CORD

26- The spring is pressed straight down, and the knot is pulled tight to ensure they are firmly tied.

27- The springs are tied together horizontally and then perpendicularly, to form a grid pattern. A slip knot is used to tie the springs and to join the cords, which will allow a certain amount of movement for adjusting the springs.

28- The fixed knots and the slip knots allow for the movement and correct adjustment of the springs and create a grid made of cord that provides a good base for the upholstery.

29- To finish, the cord is tied to the tack while firm downward pressure is applied.

30- This is the pattern of cords and springs once the task has been completed.

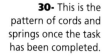

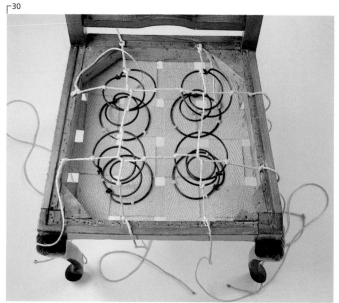

31- The correct way to set the springs is to have them lean slightly away from each other (A), because in this position, the springs become perfectly vertical when weight is applied and all provide the same resistance (B). If the tops of the springs lean toward each other (C), the middle springs will sit lower than the outside ones when weight is applied on them (D), and this would result in an uncomfortable seat.

32- Next, the springs are covered with sackcloth attached to the wood with tacks. Natural fiber stuffing is inserted and then covered again with sackcloth and attached with tacks.

33- The selected upholstery fabric is laid on the seat before it is attached permanently. This is to make sure that the pattern is centered and that the lines run parallel to the four sides of the seat. Then the fabric is carefully stretched and tacked to the wood frame.

34- The upholstery process is finished by gluing a length of gimp with all-purpose contact cement to hide the heads of the tacks. It is applied to all four sides of the seat. The fabric is protected from possible staining by placing a piece of clean paper under the gimp that is yet to be attached.

35- The result of the project is a chair that has been restored to its original condition, thanks to the help of the new upholstery.

Jewelry box

Many of the furniture pieces and objects that need to be restored are partially or totally covered with veneer or marquetry. The sheets of wood that are used in these techniques are extremely thin and fragile, and therefore can come off easily, break, and get lost, leaving bare areas. This jewelry box suffers the two most common problems of veneer: a piece that has come unglued and the loss of a small piece of veneer on one of its sides. The restoration will consist of gluing the fragment back on and repairing the area of missing veneer using a material other than wood, in this case lacquer, which will produce the same effect.

The jewelry box is made of solid mahogany, with mahogany veneer and boxwood inlay. The surface of the wood is covered with a thick layer of dark colored wax over the original lacquer, producing a matte effect. The veneer has come loose and is raised in different areas, making it susceptible to breaking and becoming lost. A small piece of veneer is missing on one side of the lid.

The interior of the jewelry box is in good condition: The hinges and the lock work well and show no signs of rust. The mirror and the velvet that covers the bottom are securely attached to the wood and the removable tray has no loose or missing pieces, but it has a thick coat of grime.

1- The restoration begins with a thorough cleaning of the surfaces of the object, beginning with the inside and ending with the outside. First the dust is removed from the velvet using a portable vacuum cleaner on its highest setting. Then, the mirror is cleaned with a commercial glass cleaner, taking care not to splash the wood.

2- A transparent commercial liquid cleaner is used on the wood surface. This product is very gentle, and it protects the wood at the same time. A cotton ball is soaked with the liquid, and the surface of the wood is gently rubbed to remove the layer of dust. Tweezers are used to hold the cotton to clean the interior of the removable tray, allowing efficient access to the corners and vertical areas.

3- Once the cleaning of the different materials inside the box is finished, the cleaning of the outside begins. A cleaner is mixed by pouring distilled water and finely ground rottenstone in a wide-mouthed container, stirring the mixture as the powder is added, until a thick paste is formed. The wood is cleaned by thoroughly scrubbing small areas of the surface, making circular motions with a cotton ball soaked with the cleaner. Next, any traces of the cleaner left on the wood are removed with a clean cotton ball.

4- Because the greatest accumulation of grime is found in the molding, in its many nooks and crannies, it requires special attention. A swab is made by rolling a piece of cotton around the end of a very fine paintbrush; the finer the better for inserting it into the molding. The cotton tip is dampened with the cleaner and used to scrub along the molding, especially in the grooves. The traces of cleaner are removed with a clean piece of cotton.

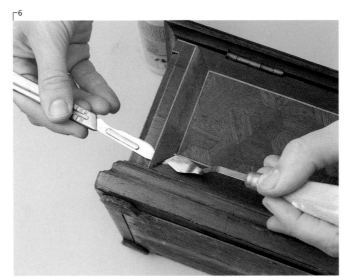

5- Neutral polyvinyl acetate adhesive is used to glue the areas of raised veneer. The veneer is extremely thin and fragile, so special care must be taken when gluing it. A small metal spatula is used to spread the polyvinyl acetate under the veneer, using just a couple of drops on the back of it.

6- The veneer is carefully lifted with a scalpel. The spatula is inserted under the wood and the glue is spread over the entire surface.

7- The veneer is held in place with a clamp, which is placed directly over the area being glued, inserting a piece of paper under the wood that has been placed between the clamp and the jewelry box. A piece of wood is also inserted between the clamp and the bottom of the jewelry box. The pieces of wood prevent the clamp from making marks on the box. The paper is used to keep the piece of wood from being glued to the jewelry box, because it is possible for some of the glue to seep out due to the pressure. The glue is left to dry for 24 hours, and then the clamp is removed.

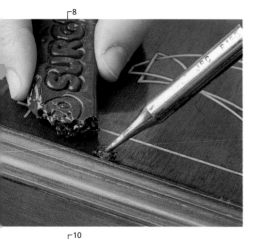

8- One side of the lid is missing a small piece of veneer. The area is too small to be repaired with a new piece, so it will be built up with lacquer. First a bar of lacquer similar in color to the wood of the jewelry box is selected. Then, the electric burn-in knife is turned on to warm up. While the bar is held in one hand over the damaged area, the burn-in knife is held closely by it with the other. This way, drops of liquid lacquer will fall to the surface and cover the area.

9- The lacquer is left to dry completely. Then, the extra material is removed by scraping with a scalpel until the lacquer-filled area is even with the wood. This task requires skill, because any slip could cause imperfections in the surface of the wood.

10- The wood used in the construction of this jewelry box is of high quality. The finish should be of the same quality as the wood and as the original finish of the object, so shellac will be used. The jewelry box is placed in a dust-free space. A couple of drops of liquid petroleum jelly are placed on the surface, and using the finishing pad charged with shellac, the wood is gently rubbed making small figure-eight motions, which will gradually become larger. The procedure is finished by wiping the piece lengthwise following the grain of the wood. Several coats are applied and left to dry. The petroleum jelly helps the pad move smoothly, making the task easier.

11- After restoration, the jewelry box displays the original colors of the mahogany and the marquetry. The combination of colors gives the piece a highly decorative look.

Writing desk

Furniture constructed of solid wood generally suffers from very specific problems. Broken parts, dents, and lost pieces are the most common. Therefore, restoration projects require, in the first place, the replacement of parts that have become detached. The most appropriate procedure will be used, depending on whether its function is decorative or functional. It is also possible that the restoration will require the repair of dents, scratches, or holes caused by rough handling. Finally, the replacement of lost pieces (molding and other decorative elements) with new pieces is one of the most usual tasks.

The restoration of this writing desk will focus on cleaning the surfaces that are in poor condition and that are stained with spilled ink, as well as the hardware; repairing detached parts and a dent; and adding a new piece of molding.

The desk is made of solid walnut with boxwood marquetry and bronze hardware. The piece has a solid structure and the exterior surfaces are, generally, in good condition. A small dent can be seen in one side, a piece of an angle in the molding of the base has come loose, and another in the same area is missing.

An examination of the interior of the desk shows that all drawers are in good condition and open and close perfectly, and the lid of the desk works well. The only problems seem to be a large ink stain in one compartment and a couple of decorative pieces that have come loose.

The finish of the exterior of the furniture piece is in the worst condition. It has been hand lacquered, which is a high-quality finish, but fragile and not resistant to dents and scratches. For this reason, the exterior, especially the top part, is in deplorable condition.

1- Before to beginning the restoration, the lid is detached and the drawers (interior and exterior) are removed and marked in numerical order. Then, the hardware is removed with a small screwdriver. The pieces are numbered and stored in individual packets together with their screws.

2- The process of stripping the outside of the piece begins. Common 96 percent alcohol acts as a solvent for lacquer, so it is used as a stripping agent. A generous amount of alcohol is applied with a brush to a specific area of the wood.

3- Next, the area to be stripped is scrubbed with number 00 steel wool to remove the layer of lacquer that is in poor condition. The task is finished by wiping the surface with a clean cotton cloth.

4- There are some insect holes, but the insects seem to be no longer active. A disinfectant is applied to each hole in the desk with a syringe as a preventive measure. A respirator and gloves should be worn in case the disinfectant accidentally comes in contact with the skin.

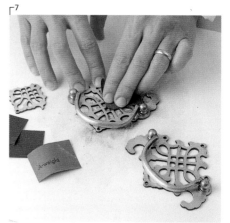

5- The elements that have been removed and the parts of the furniture that require it are cleaned. Beginning with the hardware, all of the surfaces are thoroughly brushed using a suede brush with metal bristles to loosen the oxidation and surface grime.

6- Next, the piece is dampened with alcohol to eliminate the layer of grime stuck to the bronze, and the surface is scrubbed with a metal brush until it is clean.

7- Cleaning is completed when the surface of the hardware pieces is polished with 360-grit sandpaper.

8- The surfaces of the bronze pieces are now completely clean, but they are very sensitive to oxidation because they lack the protective coating. This is why a coat of wax is applied. In a glass container, 8 fluid ounces (250 cc) of colorless wax in liquid form is mixed with a teaspoon of asphalt. It is applied using a wide brush and left to dry.

9- The surface of the hardware is buffed with a clean cotton cloth to remove any traces of wax and to give it an overall shine.

10- Finally, the brass is buffed using a brush with soft bristles to give the surface a satin shine.

11- Now, the attention is directed to the ugly ink stain in one of the compartments inside the piece. Hydrogen peroxide, a powerful bleaching agent, is used to remove it. In a thick plastic container with a tightly fitting lid, $\frac{1}{3}$ fluid ounce (10 cc) of concentrated hydrogen peroxide (30% parts per volume) is mixed with 2 drops of ammonia, and the container is closed. The ammonia will increase the bleaching power of the hydrogen peroxide. Next, a swab is made by wrapping a piece of cotton around the tip of a thin wooden stick. The tip is dipped in the bleaching liquid, and lightly applied to the stain until it begins to disappear. Then it is left to dry. It is very important to keep the container tightly closed, because both components, hydrogen peroxide and ammonia, are highly volatile and could lose their strength. The use of gloves is recommended any time that the bleaching product is handled.

12- When the wood dries out, the stain is checked to make sure it has disappeared. To neutralize the effect of the hydrogen peroxide, the wood is rubbed repeatedly using a piece of cotton soaked with tap water, and it is left to dry.

13- The water raises the grain of the wood. To remove it, the wood is rubbed briskly with a piece of 240-grit sandpaper. Next, the inside of the compartment is wiped with a cotton cloth to remove any sawdust.

14- This procedure is completed by restoring the finish of the wood. Lacquer is applied over the treated area using a wide brush. Because the wood is not stained, this application will restore the original color of the finish.

15- One side of the desk has a dent that was caused, without a doubt, by bumping the piece with another object. To fix it, a simple procedure is used, which only requires water and heat. It must be done quickly though, or the wood could be damaged. First, the surface of the dent is rubbed with a wet cotton ball, soaking the wood thoroughly.

16- Quickly, a clean cotton cloth that has been folded in half and soaked with water is placed over the area. An electric burn-in knife is set on high, and the tip is placed on the cloth, pressing hard while running it in the direction of the dent. A travel iron, without steam, can also be used for this procedure.

17- The cloth is removed to see if the dent has disappeared. To encourage the evaporation of the water on the wood, alcohol is applied to the surface with a cotton cloth. It is left to dry.

18- The water has raised the wood's grain. To remove it, the affected area is sanded by rubbing a piece of 240-grit sandpaper in the direction of the grain.

19- Next, the areas that are loose or broken are fixed by adding the pieces that are missing. First, the turned finial is attached to the base with cyanoacrylate instant glue. This type of adhesive is only used for details because changes or adjustments are not possible once the piece has been attached.

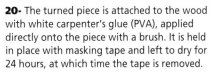

20- The turned piece is attached to the wood with white carpenter's glue (PVA), applied directly onto the piece with a brush. It is held in place with masking tape and left to dry for 24 hours, at which time the tape is removed.

21- One of the desk's front legs has several loose parts, and the upper middle piece of molding is missing. The loose pieces must be removed first. A wedge of wood is placed in the space between the desk and the piece, and the opposite end is tapped firmly using a mallet with a nylon head until the piece comes away from the table.

22- When both pieces have been removed, it is observed that each one has a nail attached that will have to come out before the pieces are glued permanently. The nails are removed by tapping on their points with a hammer until they are flush with the wood.

23- They are removed with pincers by grasping the head and forcefully pulling while making a lever motion. A scrap of wood or the two pieces of a clothespin, as is the case here, are inserted between the desk and the pincers to protect the piece from possible scratch marks.

24- Hot hide glue is applied with a thick brush over the surface that will have contact with the wood.

25- The pieces are put into place and held with clamps. Thin pieces of wood are inserted to prevent the wood from getting scratched. Also, wedges are placed between the piece of furniture and the edge of the clamp to adjust the difference in level between the various parts that form the leg. It is left to dry for 24 hours; afterward the clamps are removed.

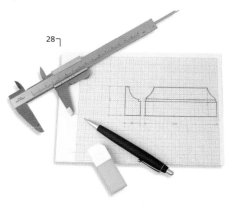

26- The center molding on the leg is missing, so one that matches the shape of the pieces on the sides will have to be added. It will be necessary to get a sample or to make a template that will be used as a model to purchase a piece of molding or to have one custom made.

27- All parts of the molding are measured with a caliper. The measurements must be accurate because any mistake could considerably change the look of the molding.

28- All measurements are transferred with the caliper to the graph paper, where a drawing of the molding is made and where all the overall measurements are indicated. The lines of the drawing are extended to make a front view and the overall measurements are indicated there as well.

29- A carpenter has made this molding from a piece of wood similar to the wood of the furniture. It is attached using hide glue and held in place with clamps (following the procedure previously described) for 24 hours. The result is a piece that fits perfectly into the angle of the desk.

30- The molding has the color of new wood, so it will have to be stained to make the piece blend with the original wood. The surface is sanded by rubbing briskly with a piece of 240-grit sandpaper. Next, water-based stain in walnut color is applied using a medium brush. It is left to dry completely.
The grain of the wood has been raised due to the action of the water in the stain. The molding is rubbed with fine steel wool or sandpaper to remove it.

31- For the finishing treatment, fine pumice powder or rottenstone is spread over the wood using a spoon or a spatula.

32- The surface is rubbed using a piece of clean cotton cloth, following the grain of the wood. This will help distribute the pumice powder over the entire surface and will help the powder penetrate the wood.

33- The original finish of the furniture is restored by applying lacquer, which is spread in layers using a finishing pad. It is left to dry. The first applications are done with small figure-eight motions, which will become progressively wider. The greater the number of layers the glossier the result will be.

34- The last layer is applied by spreading the lacquer over the length of the piece, following the direction of the grain of the wood.

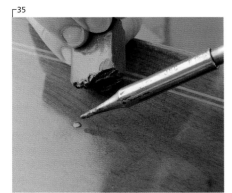

35- To finish, the holes are concealed using a bar of walnut-colored lacquer. While the bar of lacquer is held over the hole with one hand, the hot iron tip held in the other hand is placed near the lacquer until it liquefies and drips into the hole. If the drop is too large, the excess is carefully removed with a sharp tool.

36- The pieces that were removed at the beginning, such as the lid and the hardware, are put back in place. The drawers are put back into their corresponding places.

37- The result is a piece of furniture in perfect condition that can be used as a work center. The quality of the wood, which has been improved with the final treatment, constitutes the main decorative focus.

5 Renovation

The renovation of wood furniture and objects, unlike restoration, does not usually require defined processes. The condition of the object together with the level of one's ability and imagination plays a big part in the renovation process. Renovation opens a vast range of possibilities in that solutions and compositions possible are as many as the imagination allows. The addition of accessories, parts, and a particular finish are areas where solutions can be customized and personal touches can be appreciated. The possibilities are endless when renovating a piece, allowing a simple alteration in style or a complete transformation and change of function. In the following pages, you will be able to find and choose the most appropriate ones for any particular renovation project.

Decorating interiors with renovated furniture

Old furniture and objects possess certain qualities that make them special. Their style speaks of their past, and many pieces acquire sentimental value, which surpasses their market value. The good quality of the materials and craftsmanship used result in a unique and irreplaceable piece of furniture or object whose years of life and use cannot be compared to any new object.

Where to find and purchase furniture for renovating

Renovation, unlike restoration, is based on the recovery and transformation of old furniture pieces and objects of lesser status than those used for restoration. A piece or object is considered old when it is less than 100 years old and it is not Modernist or Deco in style. Its beauty and the materials used in its construction are the factors that are valued the most. The possibilities for transforming the look, structure, or function of the piece, according to the resources available and technical expertise, are also maspects to keep in mind. The individual's creativity—which adds to the personal, unique, and innovative solutions—is the only limit on the project.

Old pieces of furniture can be recovered or purchased. However, abandoned pieces or those recovered from demolitions require patient investigation before their possibilities are evaluated. Some pieces can be recovered from dumpsters or the curb where they have been left for pick up. Other places where old objects and furniture in various states of conservation can be purchased are flea markets, local auctions, and used furniture warehouses. Some warehouses located near large urban areas may have yearly liquidation sales where entire sets or individual pieces are available for purchase. No matter how furniture or objects are acquired, they must be thoroughly inspected to establish their overall condition and the possibilities for their renovation. A piece that does not offer a complete guarantee of its worth and that does not have any possibilities for transformation should never be purchased. The inspection should be based on an evaluation of the structure (if it is solid or not); the various elements such as drawers, shelves, glass pieces, and pulls; and the material from which it is made (condition of the wood and any indication of insect activity). Finally, cost, time, and effort that the process of renovation will require in relation to the quality of the piece of furniture should be kept in mind.

An old trunk has been transformed into a functional piece thanks to a creative painted finish.

Creating atmosphere with renovated furniture and objects

Renovated furniture and objects can easily become part of the decoration of any space in a house. Unlike restored furniture, renovated pieces generally have a unique flavor that is closely related to the personality of whoever performed the renovation. The main thing to keep in mind in any renovation is the creativity of the person who is doing it, because the limits are only established by technical aspects. This is why the solutions adopted will always be unique and surprising. Any renovated furniture or object will bring a sense of uniqueness to the decoration of the home. These pieces allow an array of decorating possibilities, from a fresh and innovative look, so trendy these days, to a more austere atmosphere in rooms considered traditionally more serious, such as the kitchen and bathroom.

Stripping and cleaning the door and window hardware, together with renovating the original wood, can add value to a room.

This tray decorated with a *trompe l'oeil* surface is the result of the renovation of the door rescued from an armoire.

Dresser

Sometimes a person may undertake the renovation of a piece of furniture in good condition because it has an undesirable appearance or an outdated look or because it does not match the rest of the furniture in the room. In this case, the most appropriate approach is an overall renovation combining various materials and accessories on the existing surface. The replacement of auxiliary elements—such as knobs, pulls, and molding—is an inexpensive solution that changes the look of the piece completely. Creative painting is the most appropriate procedure for changing the surface of the piece dramatically, as long as it is not in poor condition. In this particular case, the structure and the interior areas were left untouched, because they were in good condition, and the outside surface has been updated. A dresser whose surface paint was once old and had no special meaning has been transformed into a charming and lively piece, which is ideal for decorating a child's room.

The dresser is made of pine with plywood parts. Both types of materials are of lesser quality, which is why the structure is not very elaborate and the decoration is simple. The piece was painted in white enamel. The structure and the drawers of the dresser are in excellent condition. The surface paint has turned yellow over time.

1- The first step will be to remove the knobs, which will not be saved. In this case, the knobs are attached to the front panel of the drawer. They are easily removed by pulling forcefully. If any of them offers resistance, it should be tapped from the inside the drawer with a hammer and a piece of wood or any other tool with a diameter similar to the shaft of the knob.

2- The process begins by sanding all the outside surfaces of the dresser with rough sandpaper. This will remove the old paint and will prepare the wood for the new finish. When this procedure is done, the dust and the remaining paint will be wiped off with a cotton cloth.

3- The sanding operation is repeated inside the crossbars and the two frontal posts to make a smooth and clean surface free of old paint, so it will be ready for the new finish.

4- Next, the front legs of the dresser are cut off to be replaced with ones closer to the desired look. First, the dresser is turned over, making sure it is level with the floor. Then, the edge of the piece is held firmly with one hand and the leg is cut off flush with the post. The best tool to use is a back saw, held perpendicularly to the post.

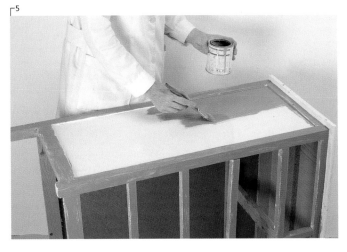

5- The surface of the piece of furniture is painted in two tones, to match the plastic border that will cover the drawers. The drawers are pulled out and a layer of turquoise enamel paint is applied with a broad brush over the entire dresser, with the exception of the top.

6- The top of the dresser is also painted with a light green enamel using a wide brush.

7- The inside areas and the rounded edges of the top panel are also painted using a thick brush with a square tip. They are left to dry.

8- The drawers are measured and then decorated with an adhesive plastic border. The length of each drawer is measured and the border is cut to fit, making sure that the motif stays centered and symmetrical with respect to the drawer. To apply the border, an edge of the protective backing is removed and placed near the edge of the drawer, pressing it by hand. Then, the backing is pulled away slowly with the other hand while the plastic is applied to the front of the drawer.

9- When this is done, air bubbles that may form are eliminated by rubbing the surface of the plastic paper briskly with the hand or with a cotton cloth, beginning at the center and moving toward the edges. Some adhesive papers can be removed and replaced within 10 minutes of their application, which allows for the correction of any possible errors.

10- The paper will be framed with a molding, which will make the drawers look more attractive. The four edges of the drawer's front panel will be measured and the measurements noted on a piece of paper.

11- The molding chosen in this case is half-round pine. A miter box is used to cut the molding precisely at a 45-degree angle. This will guarantee a perfect fit of the frame over the center of the design.

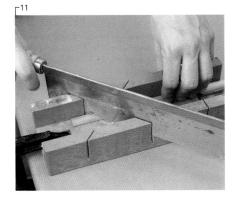

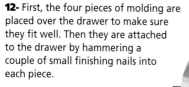

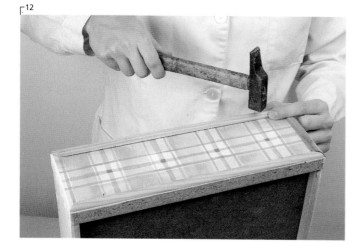

13- To conceal the heads of the nails, they are sunk with a nail set. The nail set is placed on the head of the nail and is tapped with a hammer, until the head sits slightly below the surface of the wood.

12- First, the four pieces of molding are placed over the drawer to make sure they fit well. Then they are attached to the drawer by hammering a couple of small finishing nails into each piece.

14- The holes are filled with hard wax whose color will be chosen to match the molding. A small portion is pinched from the end of the stick of wax and rolled with the fingers until a pointy cylinder is formed. The end is inserted into the hole and flattened using a wooden spatula to avoid marks and scratches.

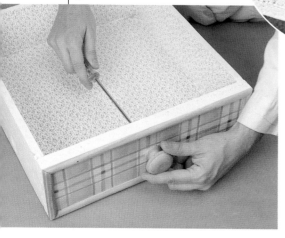

15- Knobs have been purchased to match the wood and the style of the molding. Most commercial knobs can be attached to the wood with screws, which simplifies their installation. To install the knob, a small incision must first be made with a sharp blade in the plastic over the holes where the old knobs were attached. Then the screw is inserted from the inside of the drawer through the incision and attached to the new knob.

16- Clear, synthetic varnish is applied to the wood parts, such as molding and knobs, to protect their surfaces. Several layers are applied with a medium brush, letting the varnish dry completely after each application.

17- Two turned legs, which will replace the ones previously cut off, have been purchased to match the knobs and molding. To attach them to the frame of the piece, a hole will be made in each post where the tenon of the leg will be inserted. The diameter of the new tenon is measured with a caliper, and a drill bit is chosen to fit. The dresser is turned upside down, making sure it is level with the floor. The drill, equipped with the correct bit, is centered vertically and parallel to the sides of the post, and a hole similar to the length of the turned leg's tenon is made.

18- Carpenter's glue (PVA) is carefully applied to the sides of the hole with a round, thin brush.

19- The tenon of the leg is firmly pressed into the hole. If it resists going in, a hammer or mallet with a nylon head is used to tap on the leg, holding a piece of wood in between as protection.

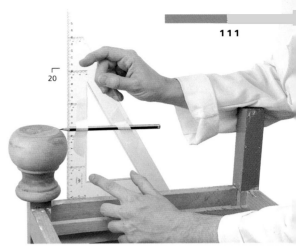

20- The back legs of the dresser are longer than the new ones, so they will have to be cut off to match. To transfer the exact measurement to the back legs, a guide is made with a 30–60 triangle, a pencil, and masking tape. The triangle's right angle is placed next to the new leg, resting on the stretcher of the frame. Then, the pencil is attached to it with masking tape so that the point of the pencil touches the base of the leg.

21- The 30–60 triangle is moved to the back leg, sliding it carefully along the stretcher. This will make a continuous line that will indicate where to cut.

22- The same procedure is repeated on the other side. When finished, there will be two lines that will serve as guides for cutting the legs straight and level. Next, the legs are cut off with a back saw. Finally, the piece is carefully turned back to its original position and left for 24 hours until the carpenter's glue dries. During this time the dresser should not be moved.

23- The renovated dresser has been given a distinctive look, and it is now very attractive. It is ideal for decorating a child's room.

Glass cabinet

The recovery and renovation of furniture can involve diverse problems. It is not unusual to find furniture whose glass components, parts, and sections are broken or missing. Replacing glass is a simple procedure (although it does require patience and a certain skill) that will surely have to be addressed on many occasions. The surfaces that are partially or completely missing should be fixed by adding sections of new wood. This case is a good example of both problems, because one of the cabinet's glass panels has to be replaced, another that is missing has to be added, and the top surface has to be repaired with a piece of plywood.

The pine cabinet with glass doors has a simple, solid structure. The wood, which originally had not been finished, is in perfect condition. The top piece of the cabinet is broken and almost completely missing. One glass panel has to be added and another one is broken. The shelves and the pieces inside of the cabinet are not broken.

1- The first step will be to remove the broken glass panel, for safety reasons. To do this, the strips of wood that hold the glass to the door will be lifted by using a screwdriver inserted between the wood and the frame and making a slight lever motion. The wood will give and come loose together with the nails that hold it in place. This is a delicate operation because any brusque movement could cause the strip of wood, which should be saved, to break.

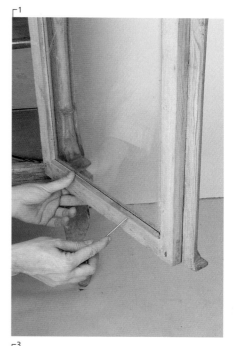

2- Next, the entire surface of the cabinet will be sanded by hand, briskly rubbing with rough sandpaper until a smooth and polished surface, free from imperfections, is achieved.

3- Then, the top panel of the cabinet is repaired by adding a piece that will cover the entire span. The area is measured and the dimensions transferred to a $\frac{1}{4}$-inch (7-mm) thick piece of plywood and marked with a pencil. It is cut with a back saw following the marks.

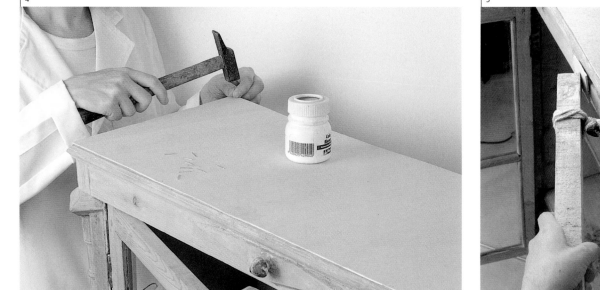

4- Carpenter's glue (PVA) is used to attach the piece of plywood to the old panel. To ensure a good bond, a small finishing nail is inserted (making sure it goes in straight) in each one of the corners and at the center of the panel's sides. It is left to dry for 24 hours.

5- The top section of the glass cabinet has a decorative finial that is to be eliminated. To remove it, a simple system is used; it will work as a lever without damaging the wood. A piece of rope is wrapped several times around the shank of the finial that is to be removed. Then the other end of the rope is tied to a large wood stick. The end of the stick should rest on the surface of the cabinet where a piece of scrap wood has been placed. The other end of the stick is pulled outward.

6- A commercial putty paste of a color similar to the wood of the cabinet is applied to conceal the hole. A small amount of it is placed on a metal spatula and applied over the hole. It is left to dry for about 2 hours and later sanded with medium sandpaper.

7- The door of the cabinet should be removed to install the two glass panels more comfortably. The screws are removed with a manual screwdriver, and the door is placed on a large work surface.

8- The glass panels (cut to size at a glass store) and the strips of wood are put together to make sure they match perfectly. Next, the strips of wood are attached to the frame with small nails. A hammer with a nylon head is used for this procedure, inserting a thin piece of wood between the tool and the glass to prevent it from breaking. When this is done, the doors are hung on the cabinet.

9- The new cabinet top is painted with latex paint (dark red in this case) using a wide brush, to blend this part with the rest of the structure. A second coat is applied after the first one dries.

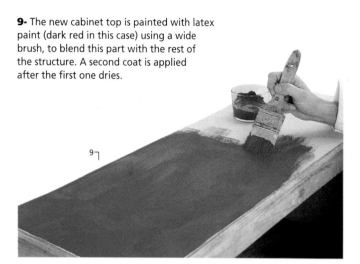

10- The interior of the cabinet and the shelves are painted as well. This is done to create contrast between the painted surfaces and the natural wood color of the rest of the glass cabinet.

11- Because the interior of the piece is very simple, it is a good idea to decorate it with designs to give it some personality. In this case, petals are used to make a design that resembles a floral motif. First, a template is made by drawing the design on a piece of paper and cutting it out with scissors. Then, it is pinned to a piece of sponge and cut out with a sharp blade.

12- Latex paint (in this case pink) is applied with a medium round brush on one of the faces of the sponge stamp. Several tests are made on a piece of paper to select the design that is most pleasing. In this case, a four-petal floral motif is chosen.

13- The interior of the cabinet is decorated by stamping the floral motif in a structured pattern. The stamp is charged, and the excess paint wiped off on a piece of paper to avoid dripping on the wood.

14- When the pink paint dries, the shelves, which have been previously painted, are put back in place. Next, the finish is applied to the exterior of the cabinet. The edges of the glass, if it is near the wood, should be protected with masking tape.

15- Several coats of linseed oil are applied to the unpainted wood with clean cotton cloths, letting each coat dry completely before a new one is applied. Linseed oil is flammable, and it can combust suddenly under certain conditions when the substance is out of the container. To avoid accidents, the cotton cloth should be rinsed in a container of water and discarded after the application is finished.

16- The door pull is attached by inserting the top screw first, lifting the pull, and then inserting the bottom one.

17- The completed glass cabinet has acquired a very attractive look thanks to the paint and the oil finish, which highlights the natural beauty of the wood.

The medicine cabinet is made of pine and painted in white enamel. The piece is in perfect condition. The only problems are the paint, which has turned yellow with time, and the scratches and dents typical of normal wear and tear.

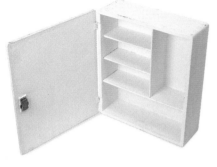

Medicine cabinet

One of the most exciting aspects of renovation is returning wood to its original condition. The look of a piece of furniture radically changes when good-quality wood resurfaces after being hidden under several layers of paint. For the most part, the original wood is in good condition, displaying a light and even color, due to the protective effects of the paint. In this instance, the warm look of the pine, the material that was used to make this medicine cabinet, will be unveiled. To add aesthetic value to the piece and to update its look, a door with a curtain will be made, using a store-bought frame rather than cutting the original door.

1- The first step of the renovation is to remove all the paint from the hinges, by scraping it with a sharp tool. When this is done, the door is removed and discarded.

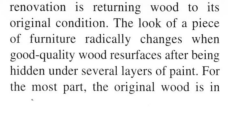

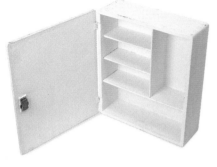

2- Next, the paint on the entire surface of the medicine cabinet is removed with a hot air gun, to recover the original look of the wood. The hot air gun is held perpendicularly to the piece, holding it at a distance and adjusting the temperature and the flow as needed. In a short time the paint will soften and form bubbles. A painter's spatula will be used to remove it. The stripped surface will be sanded with medium sandpaper.

3- A frame, like the ones used by painters to stretch canvas, is purchased to replace the old door. The frame can also be custom made. Before hanging it, the wedges must be removed from all the corners. The holes from the wedges and the joints should be filled with a commercial putty that matches the color of wood and that is applied with a spatula. It is left to dry for a minimum of 2 hours, after which time the entire frame is sanded with medium sandpaper.

4- The door is attached to the body of the cabinet with the existing hinges. To make this task easier, the cabinet is placed on a thin board, which will be slightly elevated in relation to the frame. The frame is placed next to the cabinet and the hinges temporarily attached to it with masking tape to prevent them from moving. The gimlet is inserted into the hole of the hinge and a mark is made in the wood to indicate the location of the screws. The masking tape is removed, and the screws are tightly attached to the frame.

5- A varnish filler will be used as the finish for the wood. Long neoprene gloves and a respirator should be used for protection. The varnish is applied with a cotton cloth or a rag following the direction of the wood's grain. When the last coat dries, the cabinet is sanded with very fine (400-grit) sandpaper. The final step is to rub the surface with number 0000 steel wool.

6- The opening of the frame will be covered with a curtain. First, the area where the fabric is to be placed, which will be slightly larger than the opening, is measured. The curtain is attached with two hooks screwed at the sides of the frame, slightly below the edge of the door when it is closed. The fabric should remain perfectly taut.

7- The curtain can be custom made at a fabric store. It should be mounted on a wire with rings at each end.

8- The two hooks that will hold the curtain at each end are inserted at the same height so that they will not be in the way when the door is being closed. Next, the two rings of the curtain are hung from the hooks. The procedure is repeated at the bottom.

9- Finally, a pull shaped like a star, purchased at the local hardware store, is screwed into the door's frame. The lock, consisting of a small latch hook and a ring, is attached to the door and the body's frame.

10- The new look of the small cabinet is completely different from before. Combining the color of the wood with the white of the curtain results in a fresh and updated style, which goes along with the current trends.

Chair

One of the most common problems when renovating furniture is wood that is in bad condition. Wood is by nature a delicate material that reacts to changes in humidity and temperature. That is why wood furniture left outside for an extended period of time exposed to weather, appears dry, cracked, and discolored. In some cases it looks so bad that the only possible solution is to paint it. In this example, the object being renovated is a chair whose wood is very damaged. The chair is painted and sanded to give it an antique look, which gives it a warm feeling. The woven rush seat (a delicate natural fiber) is replaced with another made of fiberboard and complemented with a cushion.

The chair is made of pine. It has a solid structure, but the surface of the wood shows some damage, having been exposed to weather for an extended period of time. The wood is dry and cracked, and the seat, made of woven rush, is broken.

1- The first step before attempting any renovation work, is to remove the old seat. To separate it from the frame, the edges are cut off with a very sharp blade.

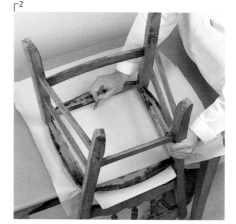

2- Once the rush seat is removed, a template is made for the seat. This will serve as the model to cut out the seat that will replace the old one. A piece of paper (in this case, packing paper) is placed on a table. Then the chair is turned upside down and placed over it. With a pencil, the inside and the outside shapes are traced onto the paper.

4- The resulting color of the mixture is a very pale pink. A coat of the primer is applied to the surface of the wood (except for the frame of the seat) with a medium brush. It is left to dry for at least 2 hours, at which time a second coat is applied.

5- Once the layers of primer are dry, the chair is painted with the selected color, in this case blue. A coat of latex paint is applied with a medium brush and then is left to dry.

3- Because the surface of the chair is in such poor condition, a primer must be applied. Commercial primers are white, so they must be tinted if required by the decorative techniques. The amount of primer needed to apply two coats to the chair is poured into a container and stirred with a long stick while adding several drops of rust red universal dye. The dye should be used with caution.

6- Next, a second coat of a different color latex paint is applied, in this case dark pink. This should be first diluted with water to give it a thin, liquidy consistency.

7- Before the paint is completely dry, the entire surface is rubbed with a natural sponge. This technique, which will add texture to the surface, helps remove the coat of pink paint, letting the blue background come through. When this is finished the paint will be left to dry.

8- To create the characteristic look of stripped wood, the chair's corners and turned pieces are rubbed with a number 00 steel wool pad. This will let the color of the primer or the wood, or both, come through. The flat pieces are also rubbed softly until the blue coat of paint comes through. Finally, the excess paint from the sanding process is removed with a cotton cloth.

9- An antique finish is used to protect the wood and to give it a finished look. Matte varnish is mixed in a container with a semidark oil paint. Care should be taken to mix in as little of the oil paint as possible, or the mixture will be too dark.

10- The varnish is applied to the surface of the chair with a wide brush, and it is left to dry.

11- A piece of ¾-inch (2-cm) thick medium-density fiberboard is cut out, using the template made of the seat.

12- This multicolored chair with a protective antique finish and new seat, is much more attractive than the original one. It has also been returned to the use for which it was created.

Corner stand

Some low-quality pieces of furniture are made with simple materials. In such cases, the renovation requires a complete transformation, changing even the function of the piece, whether it is useful or purely decorative. The transformation process often requires the use of new pieces, which can be purchased, homemade, or custom made. The most appropriate finish for this type of furniture is to paint it creatively because this will help unify all the different materials used. In this exercise, a corner stand with shelves, whose structure is very delicate, will be transformed into a hanging shelf whose function will be mainly decorative.

This freestanding corner piece with shelves is made of thin sheets of pine painted in a dark color. It is in perfect condition. Its humble structure and the simplicity of the materials makes this a fragile piece of furniture.

1- The first step is to cut off the back leg. The piece is held firmly on a work surface. A back saw is used to cut the wood, with a piece of thick cardboard between the tool and the wood to prevent cuts and scratches.

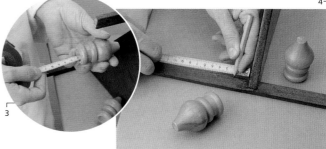

2- The cut surface is sanded with medium sandpaper to remove the marks caused by the saw and to smooth the surface. The sandpaper can be wrapped around the same piece of wood that has been cut off. This will help apply even pressure.

3- A couple of finials, which will be inserted into the front legs once they have been cut to size, are selected and purchased. The depth of the hole in the finials, where the legs will be inserted, is measured.

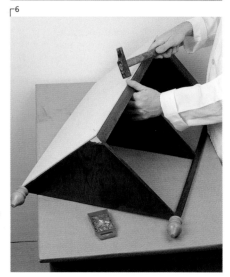

4- The measurement is transferred to the legs, beginning exactly at the edge of the lower shelf. The two legs are cut off in the same way as the first leg.

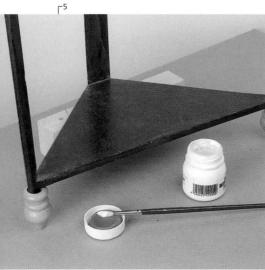

5- Carpenter's glue (PVA) is applied inside the finials, and they are put on the two legs. To ensure a good bond, the piece will be placed with the finials down, inserting a wood block under the corner where the third leg used to be. This way the weight of the piece itself will help in the gluing of the finials. The piece is left to dry for 24 hours.

6- The sides of the piece of furniture are measured. Two $\frac{1}{4}$-inch (4-mm) pieces of plywood and a third one the same width as the face of the piece of furniture are made or purchased cut to size. The boards, which will act as back walls, are nailed to the sides of the piece.

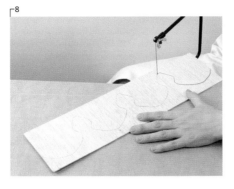

7- Two decorative skirts are made to be attached to the fronts of the two shelves. On a thick piece of paper (in this case, packing paper) a border design similar to the shape of the finials is drawn and cut out. The template is attached with masking tape to a piece of plywood, and the outline is traced.

8- The piece of plywood, placed on a work surface and held firmly with one hand, is cut out along the outline using a piercing saw. This step requires some skill, so it is a good idea to approach it with patience and care.

9- The decorative piece cut out is sanded with medium-grit sandpaper. A second identical piece is prepared following the same procedure. They are both placed on the front edges of the two top shelves as if they were hanging. They are attached using two finishing nails so they will not be visible.

10- A sealing primer is applied to the wood with a medium-sized brush, to prepare it for the final painting. The edges and corners are painted first, followed by the inside surfaces. Next, a coat will be applied to the outside of the hanging shelf and left to dry for 4 hours.

11- A second coat of primer is applied. When this is dry, the piece is sanded with fine-grit sandpaper.

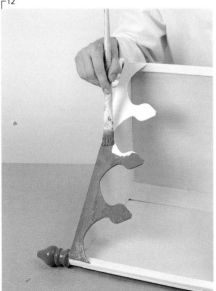

12- A coat of latex paint is applied to the inside of the hanging shelves, dark yellow in this case. When this has dried for 4 hours, the vertical posts and the decorative skirts are painted a maroon color. Finally, the edges of the shelves are painted with a checkerboard design.

13- The renovation has completely transformed the piece. It has become a hanging shelf with an oriental feeling, ideal for any corner of the house.

Side table

Renovation is not always limited to a single piece of furniture. An interesting aspect of this technique is the transformation of two pieces of furniture, or parts of them, into a single new one. Imagination and an innovative spirit are the necessary components, rather than complicated techniques and procedures. In this case, the wrought iron frame of a table with a glass top and the wood door from a library will be transformed through renovation into a side table with a country look. The two parts that will form the final piece of furniture (iron legs and door) come from two pieces of furniture of very different styles.

The library door is made of painted pine. It is in good condition, and the surface of the wood does not show any damage. The side table consists of an iron frame and legs and a glass top. The metal is in excellent condition, because it shows neither wear and tear nor rust.

1- The first step will be the removal of the metal hardware from the door: the hinges and the key hole with the pull. The door is placed on a comfortable work surface and held with a clamp. The screws that hold the pieces in place are removed with a screwdriver.

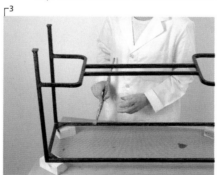

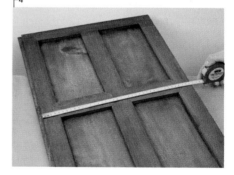

2- To conceal the holes, commercial putty, similar in color to the wood, is applied. It is left to dry for 2 hours and sanded afterward with medium sandpaper until the putty is flush with the wood.

3- The glass panel is removed from the table and discarded. Because the iron of the frame is in such good condition, the application of a finish will be sufficient. It is turned upside down on the work surface and placed on four blocks of wood, which will make it easy to reach every corner of the frame. A coat of transparent varnish made for metals is applied using a medium brush. It is left to dry.

4- The inside of the door (which will later be the tabletop) and the outside (the underside of the board) are measured. These measurements will be used to mark the underside of the door, where the iron frame will be attached. It should be centered with respect to the board.

5- The iron frame is placed on the previously made marks and attached to the wood with pipe brackets. These pieces are used by plumbers and electricians, but they are also very useful for attaching round sections to flat surfaces. Each bracket is carefully located, a hole is made with a gimlet, and then they are attached with screws.

6- When the table has been assembled, the length and width of the top are measured to order a $\frac{3}{8}$-inch (8-mm) thick piece of glass cut to fit the wood board.

7- A coat of furniture wax is applied to the wood with a cotton cloth. It is left to dry for 8 hours.

8- Next, the wood is polished using a cotton cloth and rubbing in the direction of the wood's grain.

9- Bunches of dry flowers, some of natural colors and others dyed, are purchased. The flowers are separated from the stems by cutting them carefully with sharp scissors and placing them in different containers.

10- The containers with the flowers are placed on the tabletop and different arrangements are tried in the panels to see how they balance and contrast. Finally, the flowers are placed separately in each space, spreading them to cover the area entirely. The glass panel is placed over the table. A drop of transparent silicone on each corner of the board is recommended to secure the glass and prevent it from moving, should the table be placed in an area of heavy traffic or used daily.

11- The result is a side table of a rustic style with beautiful colors and textures that give the piece an authentic country look.

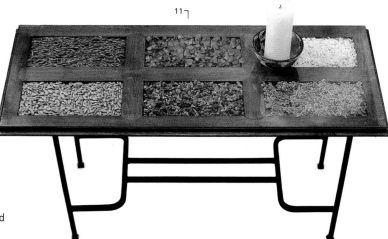

Cupboard

Recovered furniture often requires the replacement of parts and pieces and the application of new finishes as well. These are as important to the outcome of the project as is the strengthening of the frame or repairing surfaces, because the details provide a certain flavor and a finished look. In this case, the piece being transformed is a cupboard whose surface is completely covered with a coat of old paint and that is missing some parts, such as glass and several pulls. The main task will be to prepare the wood by stripping it first, and then applying a protective coat. The decoration of the piece will be achieved through the application of various varnishing techniques. New elements—such as lattice doors, knobs, and pulls—will be added to complete the look.

The cupboard is made of pine, which is thick in some areas and thin in other areas, such as the front, side, and back panels. This type of construction results in a piece of furniture of uneven quality. The structure is in perfect condition, but the coat of paint is not. Also, some of the pulls as well as the upper door panels are missing.

1- First, the shelf and the drawers are removed and then the pulls, by unscrewing them from the inside of the drawers and doors. Next, to make the job more comfortable, the piece is turned upside down. In a well-ventilated area, a coat of a commercial stripper in gel form is applied to one of the side panels. Long neoprene gloves and a respirator are recommended for protection.

2- The stripper is left on for a few minutes until the layer of paint becomes soft and thick and forms a rippled and uneven surface. The paste is removed with a paint scraper and deposited on a piece of paper.

3- The surface of the panel is rubbed with a cotton cloth soaked with alcohol to remove all traces of paint.

4- The cleaning is completed by rubbing the surface with number 00 steel wool pad, which has also been soaked with alcohol.

5- A nooker knife is used to remove the paint from the edges and corners.

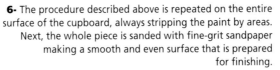

6- The procedure described above is repeated on the entire surface of the cupboard, always stripping the paint by areas. Next, the whole piece is sanded with fine-grit sandpaper making a smooth and even surface that is prepared for finishing.

7- The lower door panels are sanded rubbing with medium-grit sandpaper, because the wood on these boards is very thin and uneven.

8- The dust produced during the sanding is removed with a household vacuum cleaner set on high.

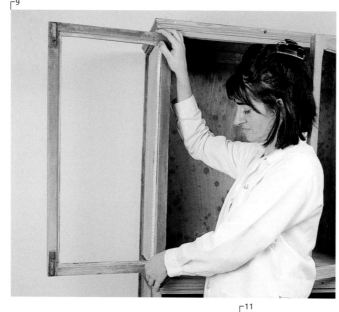

9- The panels on the top doors are missing, so two new ones made of lattice will be added. Each door is measured and the pieces are custom made by a carpenter or purchased at a hardware store.

10- The screws holding the hinges are removed with a Phillips screwdriver, and the top doors are taken off.

11- The left-hand door is placed on a work table to remove the vertical wood strip that is nailed to it. The piece is held firmly with one hand, while a screwdriver with a fine point is inserted between the door's post and the strip with the other hand, to pry the piece loose until it comes out.

12- The nails are removed with pincers by placing a small piece of wood on the post, next to the nail. The head of the nail is grasped with the pincers and pulled out by rocking the pincers on the piece of wood. This will protect the post from dents and scratches.

13- A lattice panel is placed in the frame of each door to make sure that they fit properly. Then the end of each strip of the lattice panel is nailed to the door's frame. The nails should be driven in vertically.

14- Next, the final protective treatment is applied to the wood. The various parts of the piece will be painted in different colors and textures, so the different areas will have to be protected with masking tape. First, the masking tape is placed around the sides of all the panels.

15- A glossy, cherry varnish is applied to the horizontal and vertical elements that frame the panels of the cupboard. They are left to dry, and the masking tape is later removed.

16- Masking tape is placed over the corners and the inside edges of the varnished pieces. A coat of transparent glossy varnish is applied with a cotton cloth to the side panels, drawers, removable shelf, and lower panels, to give them a textured rustic look.

17- The wood inside the cupboard is dirty and has many discolored areas. Painting it is the best solution. A muted yellow latex paint is applied to the corners and the inside edges.

18- Next, the flat surfaces are painted with a roller. The paint should always be applied beginning at the sides working toward the center of the back panel and then on the sides moving toward the front.

19- The doors are replaced, driving the screws back into the hinges. Next, a final coat of glossy cherry varnish is applied to the lattice. This step requires some attention, because all the sides of the wood strips must be painted or the finished piece will not turn out well.

20- Two drawer pulls and two knobs of matching walnut color have been purchased. A template is used to attach them to the drawers, concealing the holes of the old pulls and knobs. First, a template of the drawer pull is made by tracing the outline of its base on a piece of paper. The holes where the screws will be inserted are marked and then the template is cut out.

21- The front of the drawer is measured, and the template placed so it is level and conceals the existing hole. The locations of the holes are marked with a pencil.

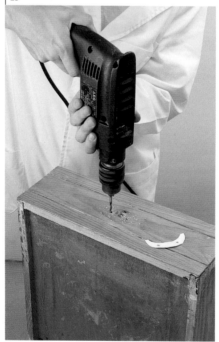

22- The diameter of the screws is measured with a caliper. Then a drill bit of a similar size is selected, a number 4 in this case.

23- The electric drill with the selected bit is held perfectly vertical when making the holes. Next, the holes are checked with the template to make sure that they match.

24- Finally, the pull is held on the front of the drawer and the screws are inserted in the holes. Then, they are driven from the inside of the drawer until the pull is firmly attached to the wood.

25- The cupboard did not originally have a keyhole. The piece has acquired a new look but this detail will need to be added to give it more class. The keyhole is placed over the existing hole to make sure it is somewhat larger. The outline of the piece is traced with a pencil.

26- The wood is removed using a rotary tool fitted with a very fine bit. The bit is placed inside the hole and moved sideways to cut the wood until the hole matches the traced outline.

27- The metal keyhole is inserted into the hole. Finally, the new knobs are attached, screwing through the existing holes in the pull out panel, located above the drawers.

28

28- View of the finished cupboard, which after the renovation looks completely different from the original. A piece of furniture that was almost beyond recovery, has been transformed into a cupboard with a bit of colonial flavor.

Stool

Transforming one piece of furniture into another with a completely different use in most cases requires changing or renovating its structure. Any change made to the structure of a piece involves complex technical procedures, which are time consuming and expensive, requiring some technical skill. However, there are some types of furniture whose look and function can be changed completely without altering their structure. In this case, a side table has been transformed into a practical stool. The process only required moving the stretchers and shortening the length of the legs. Two new side arms and a cushion have been added to make the seat more comfortable.

The side table is made of solid wood stained in dark walnut. The overall condition of the wood is good. The frame of the piece has not been altered, so it is very solid. The top is made of two pieces of wood of medium thickness, strong enough to serve as a stool.

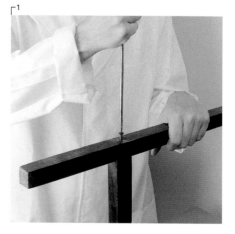

1- The first step will be to modify the location of the stretchers. These pieces serve to reinforce the structure of the legs, and they generally help strengthen the furniture piece, that is why it is very important to save them. The H-shaped frame is removed by unscrewing the short crossbars that join the legs.

2- The total height of the piece is measured, and it is decided where to cut the legs (in this case it will be one-third of their length). Next, the old mortise and its location are measured with respect to the sides of the leg. The measurements are transferred with the 30–60 triangle and marked with the point of a scalpel or a knife, at about one-third of the new height of the legs.

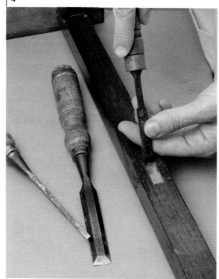

3- To make the new joint, the following easy system is used. Several holes are made close together using a drill with a number 8 bit, without piercing through the leg completely. This way a good portion of the wood can quickly be removed from the mortise.

4- Using a chisel whose blade is slightly smaller than the size of the hole, the wood is cut to the required size. The chisel is placed with the back of the blade facing out, and it is pushed forcefully, striking the handle with a hammer if necessary.

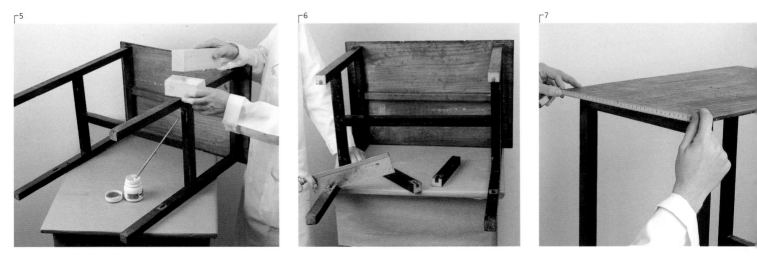

5- The stretchers are glued and set in place, inserting the tenons into the legs. The area where the bars join the legs are tapped to ensure a perfect bond, using a piece of wood to protect the surface from scratching. The glue is left to dry for 24 hours, during which time the piece should not be moved.

6- Once the stretchers have been glued, the four sides of the legs are measured and marked. Next, they are cut off with the back saw.

7- The transformation of the piece of furniture into a stool will require the addition of arms. The sides are measured first, and then two sections of pine railing are purchased at a store.

8- A dark walnut varnish is used to blend the color of the new elements with the rest. Each piece is placed on a work table on two wood blocks, and two coats of varnish are applied to them using a medium brush with a square point. The varnish is left to dry after each application.

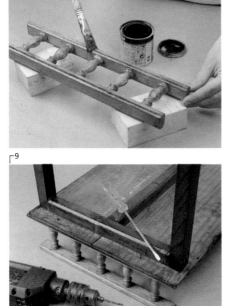

9- The pieces are attached to the stool. The sections of railing are held to the sides of the seat with a pair of clamps. The stool is turned upside down and holes are made in the board and partway into the railing, using an electric drill with a number 4 bit. Finally, the railing is screwed to the seat of the stool.

10- The completed project, which has transformed the table into a stool. A cushion has been added to make the stool more comfortable.

Table

Staining is the process that produces by far the most spectacular results. It adds new value to furniture, changing the look of the material completely without altering the inherent properties of the wood: quality, marking, grain, hardness, and so on. In this case, the surface of a table, which was finished with paint and varnish, will be renovated. First, the wood will be stripped and sanded, and then it will be stained in various colors. Masking some areas with tape will allow the creation of geometric motifs, which will be painted in different colors. In this case, the designs will be arranged on the tabletop and the front of the drawer, to resemble a border. The process is concluded by eliminating the grain raised by the action of the water and by applying a protective finish to the entire piece.

The table is made of solid pine. The piece is sturdy because its frame is in good condition. The tabletop is covered with a layer of varnish, and the wood on the drawer, sides, and legs is painted with white latex. The wood is in fair condition, considering the normal wear and tear of daily use.

1- The first step is to remove the layers of paint and varnish that cover the wood and to remove the drawer pull. Because the table is made of thick pieces of solid pine, it can stand caustic soda, which will be used in solution form as a stripping agent. In a wide, deep plastic container, a mixture is made of 2.2 pounds (1 kg) of caustic soda and 2 quarts (2 L) of hot water.

2- A cotton cloth is soaked with the solution and the liquid squeezed onto the surface of the wood. The liquid is spread over the area to be stripped, scrubbing with the cotton cloth. Next, the wood is rubbed with a number 00 steel wool pad (always following the direction of the grain) until the layer of paint has been completely removed. Finally, the wood is rinsed by rubbing it with a cotton cloth and a generous amount of water. It is left to dry.

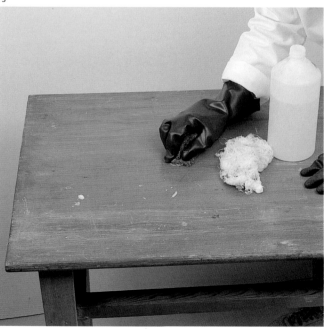

3- Alcohol is used to remove the varnish from the tabletop. A generous amount is applied to the surface with a cotton cloth, following the direction of the wood's grain. Once the alcohol has done its work, the surface is rubbed with a 00 steel wool pad until the layer of varnish has disappeared. The rest of the table is also rubbed with a cloth soaked with alcohol.

4- The wood is prepared for staining by sanding the surface with fine-grit sandpaper, following the direction of the wood's grain, until the surface is smooth and polished.

5- The staining process begins with the drawer. A piece of masking tape is measured and placed, perfectly straight and centered, over the area that is to be left unstained during the first application. This method of masking sections on the surface allows the application of different color paints.

6- The dye is prepared in a glass container, mixing tap water with water-based aniline in powder form. The amount of aniline will vary depending on the color desired. The darker the color the greater the amount of aniline that needs to be added. Because caution is recommended when using this material, only a small amount should be added at a time. The colors that will be used to stain the table are prepared at the same time: green, purple, and orange.

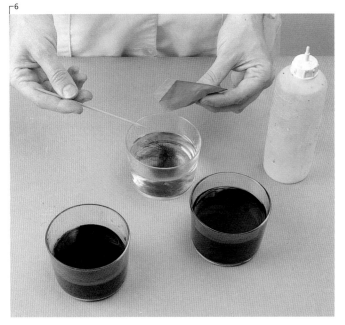

7- The green stain is applied over the surface that has not been masked, using a medium brush. Excess stain should be removed from the brush before each application or the water of the mixture could run under the tape to stain the masked sections. It is left to dry for 2 hours.

8- The masking tape is removed when the surface is dry. The stained areas are protected, masking both sides to prevent the colors from mixing.

9- The area that has been left uncovered is stained with purple paint, using a medium-sized flat brush and making sure the bristles are not overcharged. It is left to dry for 2 hours, meanwhile the drawer and the sides are painted purple. These are also left to dry.

10- A purple rectangular design similar to the one on the drawer is repeated on the tabletop. The masking tape is measured and applied carefully, keeping the same proportions as on the drawer front.

11- Orange dye is applied to the surface and underside of the table, with a lightly loaded wide brush, applying the paint evenly. If necessary, streaks and brush marks can be blended by wiping them with a cotton cloth. It is left to dry for 2 hours.

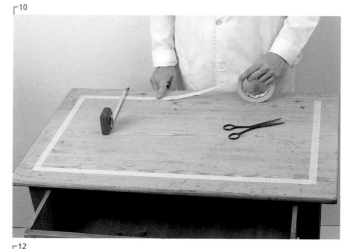

12- The edges of the orange areas are masked as described before, and purple dye is applied to the open area. The wood is left to dry completely, and then the masking tape is removed.

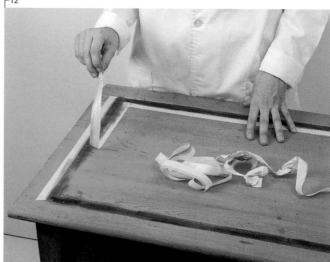

13- The wood inside the drawer shows the results of the normal wear and tear of daily use. A coat of transparent matte varnish is applied with a cotton cloth to protect it and to give it a finish in keeping with the rest of the piece.

14- An unfinished pine knob has been purchased at a store. It is stained orange and attached to the drawer with carpenter's glue (PVA). The glue is left to dry for 24 hours before handling the drawer.

15- The water in the dye has raised the grain of the wood. The entire surface is rubbed with esparto or a natural fiber pad to eliminate it. Using sandpaper would remove some of the color.

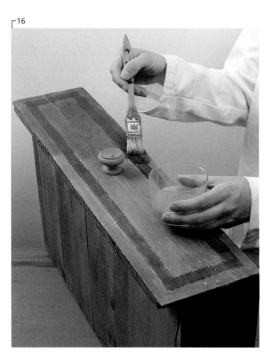

16- Now the table is ready for the finish coat. Transparent matte varnish is applied to the entire piece with a brush. The first coat of varnish is allowed to dry, and a second coat is applied.

17- A simple dyeing process has dramatically changed the look of the table. The contrast of the colors gives new life to the wood.

Storage unit for CDs

Renovation is not always limited to a single piece of furniture. Sometimes only elements or parts of one or of several pieces of furniture are used to create a new one. The recovery of certain parts and their transformation is an interesting aspect of renovation. In most cases, this will require removing or adding only a few elements, which will completely change the look and use of the piece. The following exercise illustrates the transformation of the lid of an old sewing machine into a standing piece of furniture for the storage of compact discs.

The cover of an old upright sewing machine is made of cherry and is in good condition. The coat of varnish has some scratches as a result of its normal use. The inside is not marked up at all, and the handle is firmly attached to the lid.

1- The first step is to repair the finish of the wood. The outside of the cover is stripped using 96 percent alcohol over an area and rubbing it with a number 000 steel wool pad. The remaining varnish is softened by rubbing with a cotton cloth.

2- The wood is varnished with a diluted solution of cellulose varnish. Two parts of varnish to one of solvent are mixed in a ceramic or glass container, and stirred until the liquid has a smooth consistency. Long neoprene gloves and a respirator are recommended for protection.

3- The diluted varnish is applied with a finishing pad and is left to dry. Next, the surface is sanded by rubbing it with 400-grit sandpaper first and then with a number 0000 steel wool pad until the surface becomes very smooth. Then a second coat is applied.

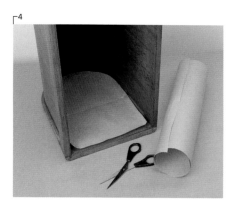

4- The addition of two shelves will be necessary to transform the cover into a storage cabinet. A template is made by cutting heavy wrapping paper to fit inside the cover. This is then used to cut the shelves from $\frac{1}{4}$-inch (1-cm) thick medium-density fiberboard.

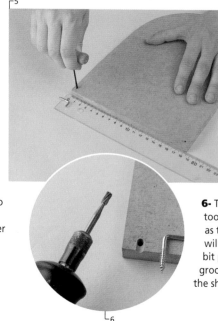

5- The front part of the shelves will be attached with a couple of L-shaped hangers, which will be inserted into holes made on the underside of the shelf to secure the wood firmly. The locations of the holes where the heads of the hangers are to be inserted are measured and marked with a gimlet, keeping in mind that the threaded end will be screwed into the wood cover.

6- The hole will be made with an electric rotary tool fitted with a cutting bit. It will be as deep as the length of the head of the hanger so it will sit flush with the wood. Using the same drill bit placed in a horizontal position, a small groove is made so the hanger will not stand out below the shelf.

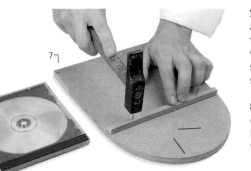

7- Two pieces of pine, $\frac{1}{4}$-inch (1-cm) square, are cut to the same length as the front edge of the shelves. Using a CD as a guide, a strip of wood is attached with brads to the top of each shelf. This will help keep the CDs lined up straight.

8- The inside of the cover is measured and divided into three sections. The locations of the hangers are marked with a gimlet, and then they are screwed in by hand.

9- The shelves are placed over the hooked nails. A template is made of the inside of each space with a medium-weight paper, as if it were a lining for the inside of the lid. Next, the template is placed over the outside of the wood and attached with masking tape. This will serve as a guide for driving the nails exactly into the back edges of the fiberboard.

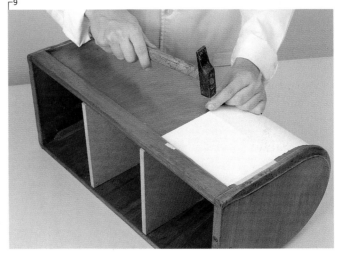

10- The base of the cover is measured and the wheels that will be attached to the cabinet are arranged. A gimlet is used to make a hole in the wood to mark the location of each wheel.

11- Two wheels are attached in the front and one in the back.

12- Two half-round pieces of molding have been stained and varnished and attached with brads to the front edge of each shelf. This will conceal the medium-density fiberboard and at the same time it will give the piece a finished look.

13- When the project is completed, the old cover will be completely transformed into a cabinet. This new piece of furniture will prove to be very useful.

Trunk

Problems encountered when renovating a wood object include insects and pieces and parts in poor condition. Insects are a common, dangerous problem, because given time they will completely destroy a piece of furniture or an object made of wood. The pieces that are in poor condition because of excess humidity, high temperatures, or both, or because they are broken, ruin the appearance of the object and can affect the solidity of its structure. The solutions to these problems are the elimination of the insects and the replacement of the parts, respectively. In this example, the transformation of a shipping box into a trunk or into a table, when the lid is closed, is illustrated. The process consists of completely disinfecting the box, repairing the insect holes, replacing the reinforcement piece that is in poor condition, and adding the elements to transform it into a trunk.

This industrial shipping box is made of pine. One side bears the old label of the manufacturer, which consists of a drawing. Its overall condition is fairly good, although the active presence of insects is detected and one reinforcement piece has rotted and broken.

1- First, the rotten piece is removed because it is beyond repair. The tip of a screwdriver is placed in between the piece and the body of the box. The handle of the screwdriver is tapped with a hammer until its tip is inserted and able to separate the board.

2- The board is removed with a strong prying motion. Because the wood is in such poor condition, most of the nails have remained attached to the box. They will be pulled out with pincers and saved.

3- A complete disinfecting treatment is necessary because the insects are still active. First, the entire surface of the box is cleaned thoroughly with a rag. A commercial disinfectant in liquid form is applied with a syringe into every hole, using gloves and a respirator for protection. This method will ensure that the liquid goes into the wood.

4- Next, the disinfectant is applied over the entire surface with a wide brush, making sure that the liquid soaks the wood and reaches every part of the box.

5- Finally, a disinfecting bag is made with thick polyethylene plastic and adhesive tape. The sides of the plastic are sealed with the tape, making sure that all holes and spaces are covered and the least possible amount of air is left inside the bag. A label with the date will be made and attached to the outside of the plastic. It is left for 15 days.

6- The bag is opened at the end of that period. The insect holes are filled with a hard wax whose color matches the color of the wood. A portion of the wax is pinched off and rolled with the fingers to form a cylinder whose tip is inserted into every hole. The excess wax is cut off with a wooden spatula and flattened so that it is flush with the surface of the wood.

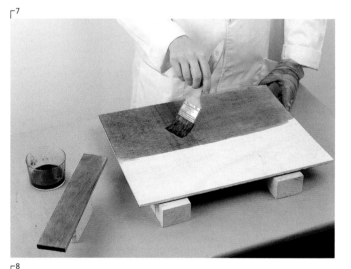

7- Two pieces of solid pine are obtained. One will replace the rotten board and the other will be the trunk's lid. These pieces are stained to match the color of the rest of the trunk. A water-based aniline dye in a light walnut color is prepared in a glass container, and applied using a wide, thick brush. When the piece is dry, the surface is rubbed in the direction of the wood's grain with a natural fiber pad, to remove the raised grain.

8- The new board is attached with the old nails. If any of these are too crooked or bent, they can be replaced with new ones.

9- Matching brass hinges, corner pieces, and a lock have been purchased. The lid is placed on the box, and the hinges are arranged with respect to the lid and to each of the sides. The locations of the screws are marked with a gimlet, and then the hinges are attached to the lid and the box.

10- Next, the lock is installed. To do this, the exact center of the lid is located, which will coincide with the exact center of the face of the box. Then, the screws holding the lock to the box are attached in the same way as the hinges.

11- A corner piece is nailed into each angle of the base. These pieces will decorate, reinforce, and protect the wood, which will have contact with the floor.

12- The handles of the trunk will be made of thick, cotton ropes to give the piece a rustic and informal look. The locations of the holes where the end of each handle will be attached are measured, making sure that they are level and centered on each side. Needless to say, both handles will have to be placed the same way on both sides of the trunk. The holes are made with an electric drill fitted with a number 8 bit.

13- The white cotton rope is inserted through one of the holes. Next, two large wood beads are threaded onto the rope handles, to give them a finished look and to protect the rope from the wear and tear caused by friction on the wood.

14- The necessary length of rope is left outside for the handle and knotted from the inside of the box, and then the excess rope is cut off.

15- A coat of walnut-colored furniture wax is applied to protect the wood and to give it the appearance of a quality piece. A cotton cloth is used to apply the wax evenly over the outside of the trunk, and then it is left to dry.

16- When the wax is dry, the entire surface is polished by rubbing with a clean cotton rag. This imparts a deep, satiny shine that embellishes the wood.

17- The new brass pieces contrast with the old wood. The surface of all the metal accessories are dyed to tone down the shine of the metal and to unify all the finishing elements of the trunk. A generous amount of asphalt is placed on a piece of thick cloth and applied to the visible surfaces of the brass with patting motions. It is left to dry.

18- The result of the renovation is the transformation of an old shipping box into an attractive rustic trunk that could be used for keeping personal belongings.

Glossary

Acetone
Colorless, flammable, and volatile liquid that is derived from the liquid produced by the combustion of wood. Used in many industrial formulas and as a solvent.

Adhesive
A substance that is used to bond two surfaces. Depending on its origin it can be synthetic, mineral, animal (glue), or vegetable (gum).

Alloy
A metal resulting from combining two or more metals when molten.

Bleaching
Changing the color of wood, usually to a lighter tone, by applying chemical substances.

Border
A strip of paper, plastic, or other material with repeated designs or motifs that is generally applied as decoration at the edge of a surface. In furniture and wood objects, the borders are usually carved in the wood.

Carnuba
A gray-colored substance that is harder and more fragile than beeswax. Extracted from a certain variety of palm tree, it adds hardness when mixed with beeswax.

Consolidate (to)
To give consistency to a material, or to reinforce it, by impregnating it with liquid adhesives or by bonding a layer of material to another.

Dowel
A small, slightly tapered, cylindrical piece of wood, that is used to hold and reinforce joints.

Drill bit
Interchangeable boring tool that attaches to drills. There are bits for drilling wood, masonry, and metal.

Frame
A group of supporting pieces on which something is constructed (such as panels in the case of furniture).

Framework
Structural frame whose interior is hollow, upon which parts are placed and attached on the sides. On a door, the stiles and rails that support the panels.

Glue (to)
To bond two parts together using an adhesive.

Gum turpentine
An essential oil, used as a medium in certain types of paints and as a solvent.

Half-round molding
Strip of wood or convex molding with a semicircular shape.

Hardware
Accessories, usually made of iron, used to adorn an object or a furniture piece.

Hinge
Piece of hardware made of two connected parts, usually steel, that rotate on a pin. Used for hanging doors in a frame, allowing them to swing.

Inlay
A surface decoration consisting of pieces of wood, bone, metal, or other materials inserted in incisions made in solid wood.

Join (to)
Attaching pieces of wood to each other using joints like the mortise and tenon.

Marquetry
Decoration on a wood surface made by gluing different pieces of wood veneers or other materials on the wood, creating a smooth, even surface.

Miter
Cut made at a 45-degree angle at the end of a piece of molding, strip of wood, or panel, for example.

Miter joint
A 45-degree angle. Joint of two pieces of molding cut at an angle, in such way that when joined they form a right angle.

Molding
Element with uniform relief and profile used as decoration. Appears in both simple and compound forms.

Mortise
Rectangular or square hole made in a piece of wood that can be joined to a tenon.

Neutral
Substance of pH 7, that is neither an acid nor a base.

Panel
Each of the flat pieces of a board that is framed by crosspieces and posts, moldings or pilasters.

Paraffin
A solid, white substance made up of a mixture of hydrocarbons, obtained by distilling lignite and coal.

Patina
Tone, color, and quality that develop on the surface of old objects with the passage of time.

Plane (to)
To diminish the thickness of a piece of wood by taking away material when cutting it. The tools that are used for reducing are the plane, the chisel, and the gouge.

Post
Vertical member of the structure or frame of furniture, to which other pieces are attached, such as the stretchers and the panels.

Skirt
Part of a board or large rectangular piece of wood that is on the lower part of furniture and that usually does not form part of the structure.

Raised grain
A group of fibers on the wood surface that stands up above the grain. They become raised when the wood is wet.

Reparation
To replace an area or missing piece.

Rush (bulrush)
A plant with long and narrow leaves that grows in wetlands. The braided leaves are used to make mats and chair seats.

Sanding
The action of rubbing a surface with sandpaper to make it smooth, polished, and free from imperfections.

Sheer curtain
Curtain made with a type of thin fabric, somewhat transparent. It is usually held with wires at the ends.

Stretcher
A horizontal member of the structure or frame of furniture that joins two opposite sections and that, in certain pieces of furniture, together with the posts holds the panels.

Stripping
To eliminate layers of paint or varnish that cover the surface of the wood.

Structure
A group of parts that, when assembled, form the frame of a piece of furniture or object. The structure supports locks, separations between components, and decorative elements.

Supersaturated solution
Solution of one component dissolved in another that cannot absorb any more and begins to precipitate.

Swab
In restoration, a utensil used to clean surfaces. It can be made at home by wrapping a piece of cotton around a long wooden stick of medium thickness.

Tarnish
Oxidation that forms on objects or parts made of metal. In some cases, depending on the type of metal, it contributes to its preservation.

Tenon
The end of a piece of wood, cut to a cylindrical or rectangular section that is narrower than the rest of the wood, which allows it to be inserted and joined to a matching hole in another piece of wood.

Tourniquet
Clamping system consisting of a thick cord wrapped around the surfaces to be held. Pressure is applied by twisting the cord with a piece of wood.

Turpentine
Essence of turpentine.

Wood borer
Parasitic insect that lives in or on wood. Some species also consume the wood.

Wood grain
Veins or fibers in wood.

ACKNOWLEDGMENTS

To María Fernanda Canal for trusting our team for this project once again. Also to Adriana Berón for her help and enthusiasm and to Joan Soto for his helpful comments.

To Marc Salvador, Sergi, Josep Pascual, Montserrat Cuadras, Isabel Juncosa, and Magda Gassó for their patience, support, and constant help.
Eva Pascual

To Miguel Patiño, Charo Garcigoy, Alba, Joan García, and Jimena Gómez for their great help. Also to Julisa Urbina for her technical collaboration in the restoration of certain pieces of furniture.
Mireia Patiño

To Sergio Milán and María Isabel Viloria for their invaluable help and collaboration.
Ana Ruiz de Conejo

Comercial Gumi
Products for Safety on the Job
Travesía Industrial, 111
08907 L'Hospitalet de Llobregat
Barcelona

Estudi de Restauració
Felip II, 227
08027 Barcelona

Els Encants del Carme
Carme, 70
08002 Barcelona

FURNITURE RESTORATION AND RENOVATION

Original title of Spanish book:
Restauración y renovación de muebles

© Copyright 2000 by Parramón Ediciones, S. A. World Rights
Published by Parramón Ediciones S. A., Barcelona, Spain.

Text:
Eva Pascual Miró

Projects:
Eva Pascual Miró: disinfecting
Mireia Patiño Coll: restoration
Ana Ruiz de Conejo Viloria: renovation

Photography:
Nos & Soto

Translation:
Michael Brunelle
Beatriz Cortabarria

English edition for the United States, Canada, and its territories and possessions © copyright 2001 by Barron's Educational Series, Inc.

All rights reserved. No part of this book may be reproduced in any form, by photostat, microfilm, xerography, or any other means, or incorporated into any information retrieval system, electronic or mechanical, without the written permission of the copyright owner.

All inquiries should be addressed to:
Barron's Educational Series, Inc.
250 Wireless Boulevard
Hauppauge, New York 11788
http://www.barronseduc.com

International Standard Book No. 0-7641-1696-7
Library of Congress Catalog Card No.: 2001088822

Printed in Spain
9 8 7 6 5 4 3 2 1

3 6058 00125 3653